ng Spe

Teaching Special Needs

Strategies and Activities for Children
in the Primary Classroom

Sylvia McNamara and Gill Moreton

David Fulton Publishers

London

David Fulton Publishers Ltd
2 Barbon Close, London WC1N 3JX

First published in Great Britain by
David Fulton Publishers 1993

British Library Cataloguing in Publication Data

A catalogue record for this book is available from the British Library

ISBN 1-85346-247-0

Designed by Almac Ltd., London

Typeset by RP Typesetters Ltd., Unit 13, 21 Wren Street, London WC1X 0HF

Printed in Great Britain by Bell & Bain Ltd., Glasgow.

Contents

List of figures

Introduction

Whilst this book is primarily about a teaching approach for all children in the primary classroom, it is also about a teaching approach which enables children with special needs of all descriptions to flourish and make discernible and significant academic progress. It is important for teachers to understand the possible links between their own behaviours and belief systems and the academic behaviours and achievements of their pupils, therefore the rationale that the authors work with is carefully laid out below.

Some of the methods and strategies in this book are derived from counselling psychology and may be familiar to you from personal and social education. It is our experience that if these approaches are left in the P.S.E. curriculum the children are unable to transfer them to other areas. Many teachers feel that these skills and attitudes are very important to their work in the classroom and to the social life in the playground. In this book we develop an approach which combines skills teaching within and through the subject curriculum. Our experience is that when this happens the children can transfer the skills more easily. This is of benefit to all children but is particularly important for children with special needs.

CHAPTER 1

Why Include Children with Special Needs?

In this chapter we explore:

• the rationale for integrating children with special educational needs into the mainstream primary classroom.

• the relationships between self-esteem, attribution theory, learned helplessness and children with special educational needs.

• the traditional approaches to teaching children with special needs.

• the importance of peer tutoring for integration and the curriculum.

• the role of group work for integration and teaching the National Curriculum.

• a new role for teachers in the integrated classroom.

• the process of assessment for the National Curriculum.

Integration and segregation

Since the 1981 Education Act there has been an increase in the tendency to integrate children with special needs into mainstream schools. This follows a pattern of moves towards mainstreaming in both the U.S.A. and Australia. The tendency is based on parental and societal feelings of 'normality', that is to say a belief that children make better progress when they feel they are the same as others rather than different. Clearly this is not straightforward because a child who is blind, deaf or who has cerebral palsy will probably look or sound different to other children. Parents, teachers and others may want to protect that child from the taunts or verbal insults of his or her peers in the mainstream setting. Additionally there may be an assumption that such children will progress better academically in a small group setting with specialists around them.

These feelings and assumptions are challenged by the view that children who go to a different school, particularly one labelled special, suffer from taunts from their peers when they do come back into contact with them. It is interesting to note that when some young boys at a residential special school in Leicester were interviewed about their feelings about being there, they said that they tell their friends they go to boarding school, and that their parents pay for them. Clearly some differences have more credibility than others!

The latter set of views is also supported by research and curriculum observations. Research demonstrates that children with special needs in both mainstream and special settings tend to have lower self-esteem than their peers with no special needs. Lund (1987) found this to be so whilst working with children in a special school for emotional and behavioural difficulties. Gray and Richer (1988) found that low self-esteem was the key reason for disruptive behaviour in mainstream schools. Gurney (1988) in his review of the research on self-esteem confirms that children with learning difficulties have a lower self-esteem than their peers. It has been found that whilst the self-esteem of pupils may increase whilst they are in the special school setting (Lewis 1971) it may even diminish when the child enters a post 16 mainstream setting.

Segregation may be seen not only as ineffective in increasing pupils' feelings of success and 'sameness' but as serving to increase the differences between children with special needs and their peer group. It would appear that many young people who have spent their schooling years in special schools become so compliant and dependent upon the special treatment and regime available there that special programmes of advocacy need to be drawn up for them. Indeed one colleague in further education found he was starting advocacy work with choices of coloured felt tip pens, because the student had no experience of making a choice. Everything — clothes, food, activities — had been chosen for him in his previous special educational setting.

What is also clear is that children with special needs cannot simply be placed in a mainstream setting in the hope that the normality will rub off on them. The research evidence of Lalkhen and Norwich (1990) who conducted a small scale research project using 39 students with physical needs, showed that integration does not necessarily result in high self-esteem. It is clear then that for integration to help to move children who are special into a situation in which they become more 'normal' and where their self-esteem is raised, something must be done to support that happening.

The common practice in mainstream schools integrating children with special needs is to provide for and protect children's needs by giving them special adult help. This might be an ancillary helper, a support teacher or a nursery nurse. We will argue that this does not necessarily raise children's self-esteem in the integrated setting. It may in fact compound low self-esteem.

Young adults with special needs are beginning to speak out against the amount of intervention they receive in special school settings. It seems that the level of intervention experienced by some pupils (and adults) with special needs is felt to be unnecessarily high. Their perception is that the high levels of support appropriate for those with the most severe difficulties are commonly given to all. For some pupils this support can actively inhibit their progress. The reasons for this can be seen through studying the theories of self-esteem and learned helplessness.

Self-Esteem

in creases

and achievement

It is important to note the very close correlation between a person's self-esteem and their academic and social progress. Long-term research demonstrates that a healthy self-esteem is vitally important to the long-term development of a person throughout their life (Coopersmith 1967, Burns 1982, Hamacheck 1986). It is very important to consider this correlation when looking at a group of people who have been shown to have low self-esteem — that is, those pupils who have special educational needs. In order to help these pupils to progress academically and socially their self-esteem must be considered as influential in that process. Many writers see a connection between low self-esteem and failing (Lund 1987, Lawrence 1987, Gurney 1988, Burns 1982). The effect of failure upon self-esteem is outlined below.

Self-esteem has been defined as a personal judgement of worth, lying on a continuum which has *positive* at one end and *negative* at the other (Cottle, 1965). We have pictures of ourselves which have been described as the ideal self and the perceived self. The ideal self is the person we wish to be. This will be based upon the opinions and expectations that we have picked up from those around us. The perceived self is the picture we have of ourselves based upon the information that those around us give to us. Our self-esteem is based upon the degree of correspondence between the ideal self and the perceived self. It is our evaluation of the discrepancy between the two. If we evaluate the difference as 'normal', 'close enough', 'nothing to worry about' then our self-esteem is likely to be healthy. If we evaluate the difference between the ideal self and the perceived self as 'not normal', 'vast' and ' something to worry about' then the self-esteem will be low or unhealthy.

In his definitive sub-scales Coopersmith (1967) showed that there are different types of self-esteem and that these can be measured, which he did using a self-esteem inventory and sub-scales. He defined these as global or general, personal, social and academic. All of these can be affected by a child's educational setting but the academic self-esteem is most pertinent here. In his review of the literature on self-esteem Burns (1982) quoted numerous studies showing a high correlation between academic self-esteem and academic success. White (1990) says that children who feel good about themselves learn more easily and retain information longer — in fact, they do better in every way. How can teachers ensure that pupils feel good about themselves academically in order to foster this healthy academic self-esteem and with it academic success? The answer must lie in ensuring that the feedback children receive promotes a belief that they are academically successful.

Academic self-esteem

The work by Lawrence, which was begun in 1973 and has been successfully repeated over the last 20 years, shows that an improvement in reading performance can be achieved through counselling (Lawrence, 1973, 1987). The level of improvement thus reached can be greater than that produced by more traditional remedial reading programmes, or the results achieved through remedial reading and counselling combined. This must cause teachers to ask how counselling could achieve results where remedial programmes fail. The research found no causal relationship between general self-esteem of pupils and their academic achievement but there was a clear relationship between academic self-esteem and academic achievement. The reason for the success of the counselling programme over more traditional methods appears to be the boost given to the subjects' self-esteem, particularly their academic self-esteem.

For some pupils there are factors in their home environment which may affect their achievement in school. When questioned about the causes of delinquent or difficult behaviour many teachers and others say home background, social class or housing neighbourhood are to blame. This perception might well influence the academic progress of a child in school. It is true that the home background is the reason often given for poor reading skills. This might be qualified by statements about children not having enough books in the home or that there is poor reading modelling by adults. The attitude that a child shows towards school and education might also be influenced by parental experience and expectations. A 'poor' attitude may show itself as lack of motivation and application within school. The result of any or all of these home environment influences can be a low teacher expectation, with all the implications of the self-fulfilling prophesy (Rosenthal and Jacobson, 1968). A cycle of failure can soon exist for such children, as it can for children with other 'difficulties', whether they are social, emotional or medical in origin.

Giving positive feedback

Self-esteem theory would suggest, however, that there is a way out of this cycle of poor home background leading to school failure. Coopersmith (1967) and Whylie (1979) showed that there are three major sources of feedback for children at school and each is held to be of value. These sources are the parents, the teachers and the peers. The authors of this book believe that this is a crucially important piece of research for the reasons outlined below.

The research demonstrates the power of feedback upon the self-esteem and subsequent success of students. It suggests that if the teacher can harness their own feedback and that of students' peers so that all students receive genuinely positive feedback in school, this can outweigh any negative feedback from home. Indeed it is our experience, through working with many teachers on small scale projects, that once the cycle of negative self-esteem (with its attached poor academic achievement and poor social and classroom behaviour) is broken, then parents start to come into school delighted with the changes in their child's attitude to school and motivation. As a result, the parents' own feedback may well start to change.

Children with special needs have received continuous feedback from a variety of sources that they are different. They may also have a picture of themselves as inferior, and so 'special' that they are in need of extra help and different provision. The authors believe that changing the feedback these pupils receive from 'in need of special help' to 'we are all different but equal' can change their perceived self. Feedback that promotes 'different but equal' needs to pay attention to the different strengths of each individual and show that there is real interest in everyone's contributions and ideas. Through the acknowledgement that what they have to offer is valued in school, pupils can gradually change their self view from 'I am a complete failure at school' to 'I am OK at school, although I need help sometimes with reading'.

Reading failure and low self-esteem

Lawrence's (1973) findings showed that using a counselling skills approach with reading failure achieved great improvements in reading skills than remedial reading tuition. Many teachers may well assume that it was to do with a poor reading method. This is an understandable reaction from teachers whose job it is to support children with special needs or to teach slow readers in a withdrawal situation. Another answer seems to lie in the research on learned helplessness and attribution theory.

One of the results of having low self-esteem is a tendency to give up. The authors recognise this tendency in themselves in skill areas where they feel less confident and so low in esteem, that there is very little motivation to even try. The thought processes that operate are something like:

Oh I'm no good at this... It will never work... There's no point in me trying because it never does work... It's bound to end up in a mess... Everyone will be cross and disappointed... I'll feel bad about it... So I'll get someone else to do it... It will be quicker.. Everyone will be happy.

Children do not come in to primary school with low academic self esteem. Until coming to school there has been little or no chance for them to compare academic performance with their peers and they have encountered few whom they see as knowing about their academic performance. They form a picture of themselves based on the feedback they get from teachers and peers about what happens in school. One major event in school, and one that pervades all other activities, is the business of learning to read and write. If a child does not make quick progress with reading. Children look around and begin to see that reading is not just one subject like art or playing in the water; they accurately make an assessment of themselves and see that failure in reading means failure in all academic subjects. This is because all the other subjects are delivered through reading and writing. This tendency to deliver through reading and writing starts very early and is firmly established by year three. It increases through the years until secondary school where the diet can be up to 90 per cent reading and writing.

Chapman, Lambourne and Silva (1990) showed that children's reading ability correlated to their self-esteem. This correlation indicates that children are receiving strong messages about the importance of reading as a fundamental skill and one which is central to their future academic achievement.

We have noticed the tendency to deliver the curriculum of history, geography and science through reading and writing. This has been even more noticeable since the National Curriculum was introduced, as a way of coping with the vastly increased workload of teachers and children in primary schools.

Many teachers at this point say, 'Well, that is how it is, we have to teach them to read because it is a life skill'. Whilst the authors of this book do whole-heartedly and actively work for fluent literacy for all, we feel that the way reading and writing is used as a medium of instruction for all other subjects is totally disproportionate to the communication skills required and utilised by industry and in wider society. There is little evidence that reading and writing are the most commonly used communication skills once children leave school. There is evidence that it is the spoken word that is used more often.

What we have found, through our own work with children and through working with teachers on similar projects, is that it is the very emphasis on reading skills that holds children up in their academic progress. Concentrating on the areas of weakness means that children who find it difficult 'close down'. They develop strategies to avoid trying, avoid working and thus avoid failing. The result is that poor readers become less and less motivated to become historians, geographers and scientists. Teachers' perceptions that those who can't read are not very bright at anything are thus confirmed.

Attribution of success

Traditional remedial approaches have worked towards increasing children's reading skills through small steps and approaches designed to ensure success and progression. For many children with learning difficulties, both those in the mainstream and some in special schools, this way of ensuring success is ineffective in producing real progress. This is because they are not failing because they can't learn, as they may have been at the beginning, but because they don't want to try because they don't want to risk failure. They have learnt that they don't like the feeling of failure so they would rather not try, just in case they fail again.

Some deal with failure by attributing their lack of success to sources other than themselves. They might tell themselves it was because the book was too hard, the teacher didn't tell them properly, they are tired, the others were making too much noise ... or any other factor that might be seen as having an influence. Some children certainly try to deflect the cause of failure from lack of ability or skill by behaving badly so that both the teacher and the child can attribute lack of success to bad behaviour.

Failing readers can also protect their picture of their perceived 'failing' self by believing that any success in reading is due to luck rather than effort. This denial of the part they have played in their success is based upon the way they cope with their continued failure. However this means that they fail to attribute their successes, so carefully planned by the supportive teacher, to themselves. So such success cannot raise their self-esteem nor change their view of themselves as a failing reader. They might also attribute their success to the skills of the teacher rather than their own effort or ability with similar effects.

Attribution theory suggests that children with low academic self-esteem attribute success to luck and failure to lack of ability; those with high self-esteem will attribute success to effort and failure to bad luck, or lack of effort where appropriate: 'I did not revise enough' for example. Research by Marie Louise Craske (1988) has shown that children can be trained to change this attribution of success to luck by concentrated skills training programmes. We have achieved the same results using the programme in this book. If no intervention takes place, then learned helplessness becomes a constant way of behaving. This state was originally identified by Abramson and Seligman (1978). Craske (1988) defines it in this way: 'A state of Learned Helplessness is reached when an individual perceives he lacks control in obtaining a desired outcome. The type of explanation (attribution) the individual makes for his lack of control determines the features of his helplessness.'

Skaalvik (1990) comments that individuals attempt to protect and enhance their self-esteem by taking credit for their success and denying responsibility for failure (i.e. self serving attribution). In such a situation learners may well make good progress when a support teacher or other adult 'encourager' is sitting beside them but they will continue to believe that they cannot do the work by themselves. Indeed the very presence of the support teacher or other helper confirms their low self-esteem and contributes to the cycle.

It is our belief that such a cycle cannot be broken by adults, that the way forward is for the adults to control, alter and structure the classroom, as outlined in this book, to provide an alternative learning environment. This would include an emphasis on oral work rather than reading as a key medium for learning and assessment of understanding. When writing is an appropriate way of recording the outcome then it is done with structured peer support, rather than adult support. There should be structured, specific, consistent and positive feedback for all, but especially for those with special needs, from both peers and adults.

Learned Helplessness

One of us recently sat at a table of six year 2 boys who, after an oral sharing of words beginning with 'kicking K', were required to draw the ones on the board and write the word underneath. One alert, talkative boy pointed to another quiet, reticent one and said, 'He won't be able to do this. He can't write and he's slow. He'll never finish, and he wets his pants. He's a baby.' This for me was an example of the reason why the quiet boy did no work at all unless coaxed into it by me. The talkative boy continued to say that I shouldn't be helping him as that was cheating. Doubtless if measured, the reticent boy's self-esteem would be found to be rock bottom! He had certainly learned to be helpless.

This learned helplessness syndrome may account for the dependent, passive behaviour of some students in special school settings and perhaps for the success of methods carried out by some 'alternative' institutions. It is possible that the reason for the success of conductive education is linked, in part, to the teachers' and helpers' belief that the children they take into their programmes will walk. Such teachers have high expectations of their students and so work towards independence, reducing the possibility of learned helplessness.

It is possible that the behaviour of some teachers and assistants in some special schools may be compounding the cycle of low self-esteem and learned helplessness, if they have low expectations and so do too much for the students.

It is the thesis of this book that such teachers could be engaged in structuring activities to increase independence and self responsibility. They could do this by utilising the peer group in talking, helping and tutoring, in the way advocated here.

Importance of talk for children with special needs

It has long been accepted that talk should be the means of instruction in the early years. But, probably because of particular interpretations of Piaget's work, it has been assumed that children should move increasingly towards reading and writing as a means of instruction. Consequently there are fewer expectations of talk in years 6 and 7 and a much greater emphasis on written language. Research has also shown that even where children are grouped together around tables there is little on task meaningful communication going on (Galton, Simon and Croll 1980). There is evidence that the majority of talk that goes on in classrooms is teacher talk. Flanders (1970) established by his research the 'two thirds rule'. This is that two thirds of the time available in a lesson is talk and two thirds of that talk time is teacher talk. This has been borne out by local studies in Leicestershire in both mainstream and special schools. When the student time is further analysed the amount of time a student with special needs takes for talk can be as little as one minute a week.

As can be witnessed in many classrooms, teacher talk is mainly transmitting information, giving instructions or feedback (Sutton 1981). Vygotsky (1987) and Bruner (1986), unlike Piaget (1959) and Skinner (1969), see the development of children's language as interactive rather than linear and mimicking. This means that children need opportunities to be question posers, summarisers and feedback givers if they are to develop the kinds of skills needed to be effective communicators. They need these communication skills to be group members and effective speakers and listeners, as identified in the National Curriculum (especially English Attainment Target 1). However communication through talk is not confined to the English curriculum. These skills are identified time and time again both in the statements of attainment and the programmes of study in English, maths, science, technology, geography, history, music, art and P.E. Terms such as *describe, show understanding, question,* and *discuss* occur many times throughout the curriculum documents.

Talk, however, is not just a way of demonstrating what you know, it is the way in which we actually learn. Vygotsky (1987) and Bruner (1986) both believe that language acquisition has its roots in social processes and that it is through exploratory talk that children develop concepts. This has been supported by later writers (Tann 1991, Wells 1985, 1986). Barnes (1976) puts it this way, 'Bruner and Vygotsky see language as both a means by which we learn to take part in the life of the communities we belong to and ... as a means by which we can actively reinterpret the world about us.' It would seem that even if each of these theories is only partially correct, student talk has a vitally important part to play in both the cognitive development and the interpersonal relationships of children.

If we return to the link between self-esteem, sense of failure and children with special needs, it would seem that lessons where the session begins orally, where everyone gets a chance to be listened to and be encouraged by their peers, would provide the situations where children with special needs will flourish, and this is indeed the case. In fact many of our teachers have been pleasantly surprised at the degree of maturity and independence children with special needs have displayed in such situations.

This begs the question 'If talk is so important why then is it not employed more often?' Part of the answer is because children do not readily display their skills if they have had little chance to practise them — hence this programme. It is in part because of a set of views about what is a 'special curriculum' for 'special needs'.

The special needs support teacher

Traditionally a special needs curriculum was seen as one which concentrated on the basics and taught to clearly defined targets or objectives. Unfortunately this led to a restrictive curriculum which the National Curriculum is now challenging. It also meant that remedial teaching in withdrawal groups in mainstream settings was based on the same principles, despite the fact that many children showed no signs of being remedied and simply got further and further behind their classmates.

Since the 1981 Education Act and the resultant tendency to place children with special needs in mainstream primary classrooms, there has been an interest in the process of statementing children with special needs. Statements have become a way of accessing extra resources, especially that of extra adult time for support in the classroom. As the number of children with statements increases, the whole focus of special education has become resource led, through the statementing process. As the financial climate has changed with the introduction of Local Financial Management of schools, so the anxiety about dealing with children who have special needs in the mainstream setting has increased. It is our view that it is not only possible but better, to deal with children with special needs from a class management model than from a resource led model.

Support teachers are now left in an interesting position. They can sit beside the child with special needs, interpreting the curriculum as delivered to the rest of the class for them. This is problematic as it might lead to increasing feelings of helplessness and difference. Alternatively they can try to help the classroom teacher to devise different worksheets or tasks to meet the needs of various ability levels, including the level of the pupil whom they support. This is commonly known as differentiation by task. Some teachers might feel that it is more profitable to give the child who has difficulties a differentiated curriculum of basic tasks; more reading practice, more phonics, more handwriting, copy writing, all of which are carefully graded or broken into small steps which can ensure success for the learner — the belief being that practice makes perfect and small steps ensure success. However, this approach can also unfortunately contain the hidden curicula message that the child with special needs is different and can't do the work without a special teacher providing easy work. Children learning by this approach are unlikely to attribute any success to themselves.

There is therefore a need to deliver the same curriculum in the same way for all the children but to ensure success for everyone. Indeed writers like Swann and Booth (1987, 1988) have been urging a change in curriculum delivery for a long time, arguing that the problem lies at least as much with the curriculum delivery as with the child.

There are, however, some excellent aspects of special curriculum and pedagogy which it would be foolish to do away with. These include practices such as target setting, breaking the task down to manageable steps, recording success and reviewing progress, criterion-referenced curriculum and assessment. It is our view that these excellent practices can be structured so they are taught to the children in the class and then employed by them in their learning. This would mean that children would be teaching each other and using the special 'small steps' techniques with each other.

Peer group support?

If the answer to dealing with children with special educational needs is not exclusively the use of support teachers then we have to ask, What is the alternative?

Teachers of children with special needs often talk about their experience of these children as being very demanding and requiring constant attention. It would seem that this is the rationale for encouraging the use of support teachers in the classroom. However, within the classroom there are many others who could be offering this one-to-one support and attention. The child's peer group are constantly there; many would be both able and willing to provide the support if only the teacher would both sanction this through praising this type of effort and systematically teach the pupils the necessary skills.

While peer tutoring is increasingly being used in primary school it is usually used for cross-aged tutoring of reading, with the most able and oldest students teaching the very youngest. This has clear benefits. Topping (1988) and Goodlad and Hirst (1989) demonstrate that the increased time on task, motivation and support given through having a peer tutor, lead to increased success in reading. Bloom (1984) found that the average peer tutored pupils performed better than 98 per cent of the pupils of the control class.

There is another way of organising peer tutoring. Some teachers have drawn on the research outlined in Topping (1988) which shows that as well as offering benefits to the tutees, peer tutoring raises the skills and self-esteem of the tutors dramatically. Goodlad and Hirst (1989) showed that when students with learning difficulties acted as peer tutors for their mainstream peers then both groups gained from the peer tutoring situation.

Thus peer tutoring can be an excellent way of breaking the cycle of low self-esteem and low academic achievement of children with learning and other difficulties. Many of the teachers with whom we have worked say at this point that they can't think of anything that their children with special needs are good at, so therefore they can't see how their students can become peer tutors. There are several solutions. The easiest is to find tutees who are either younger or those who have greater learning difficulties or both. However, although this might solve the immediate short term problem, it creates a problem for the recipient group, who themselves will need to experience being a tutor and benefiting from the resulting increase in self-esteem. Therefore in the longer term it is better to use the elements of this programme which encourage students to identify their strengths and state these openly in the group. In such a situation other class members can identify and use the skills which children with special needs themselves say they have. Details of how to put this into practice are given within the later sections of this book.

Teaching children the skills for peer tutoring

The skills of the support teacher, in understanding the difference between support and 'doing it for them' can also be taught to the children.

As all teachers know, researching and explaining a piece of knowledge or a concept to another person (or class) is an effective way of increasing your own understanding of the topic. There might be a concern that peer tutoring will be a waste of time for the bright child, always being on the giving rather than receiving side of the partnership. If the model is one of the brighter children 'doing it for them' then this might be the case. If however, the style is to explain, encourage and support independence in their tutee, as advocated in this book, then it will not be the case. Indeed, in our experience, all such bright children gain vast increases in their own performance, sometime suggesting that they might previously have been underachieving.

In addition, it is sometimes the case that bright children are themselves excluded by the other children and called names such as boffin, teacher's pet, etc. They may experience difficulties in forming friendships in their peer group. Peer tutoring can break down these barriers and encourage relationships with more 'street wise' children. It is often the case that the lack of social relationships in school actually disables bright children in school and causes them to deliberately underachieve in order to fit in with the group. There is a need, therefore, for the bright children to be in a tutoring relationship as a tutee. Neglected areas for peer tutoring such as art, drama, P.E. or swimming can be useful for this.

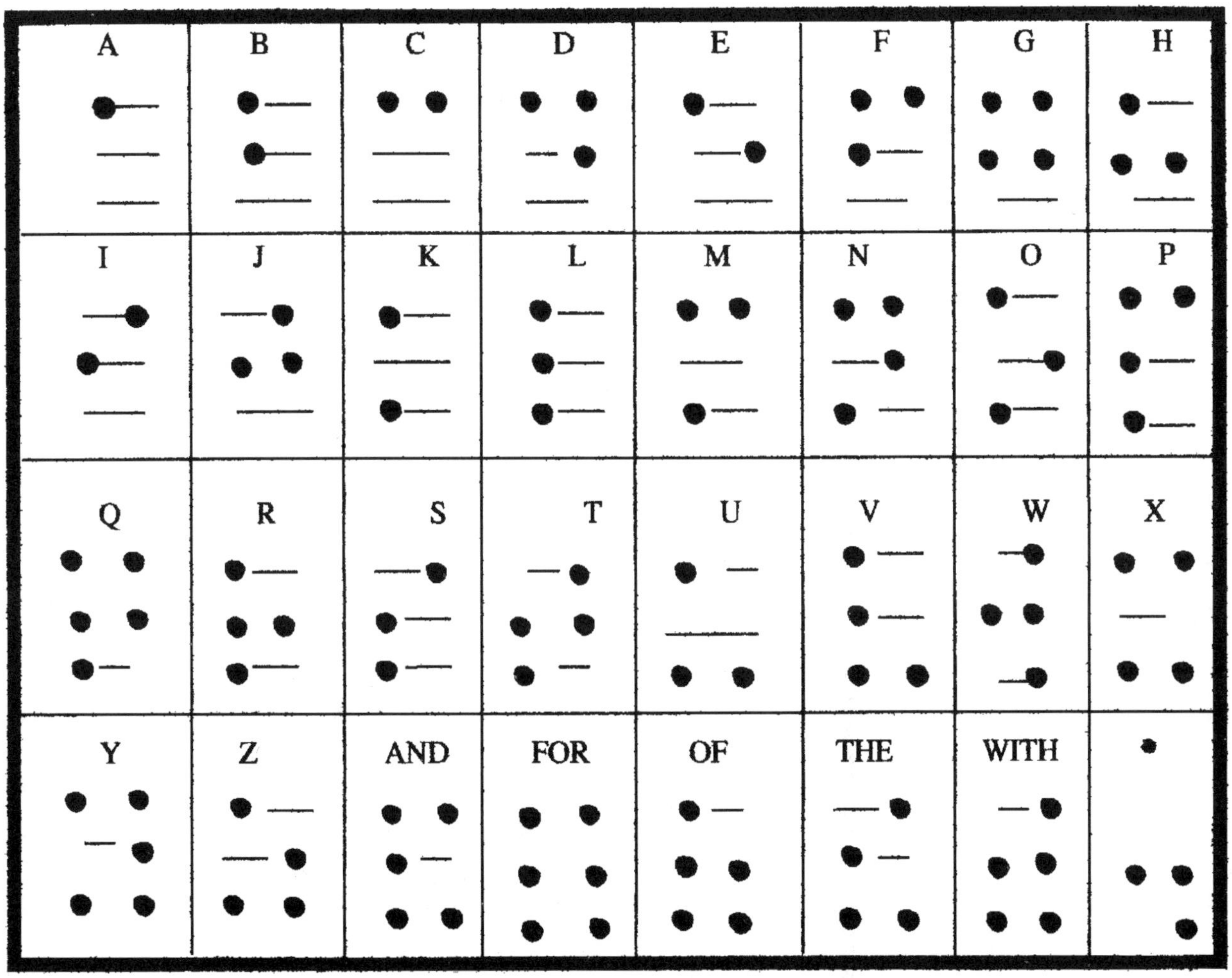

Figure 1:1 The Braille alphabet

Communication for children with special needs

For some children with particular difficulties specific skills may be required, e.g. braille. The Perkins Brailler can be used and understood by sighted peers of blind children, allowing the blind child to 'teach' their skills to the sighted child, and the sighted child can then access the work of their blind friend. This allows the traditional role of the braillist support teacher to be far more flexible in supporting all of the children in the class. This in turn will enhance learning for their supported child through allowing smaller groups within the class.

One of the authors, who had two blind children in her class, allowed the children to teach both her and her class the braille alphabet. They began sending each other braille messages, with traditional raised dots produced by the Perkins Brailler or with dots produced simply by pressing the point of a pair of compasses into stiff paper. The blind students were particularly thrilled when their classroom teacher was able to read the message that they had sent in braille, without it being transcribed.

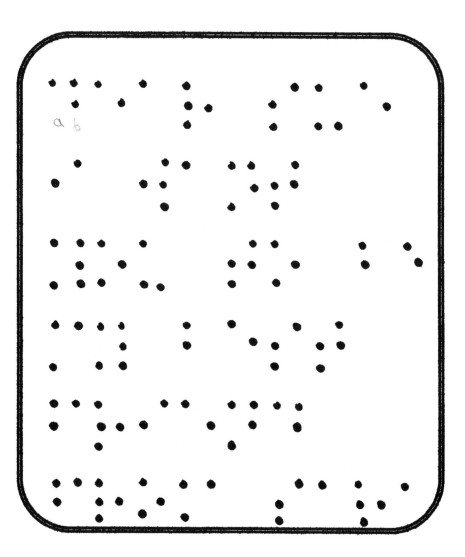

Figure 1:2 A Braille message

Children who use sign language for the deaf or 'Makaton' or other sign languages, can be supported in the same way. The child themselves or their signing teacher can teach the class teacher and the rest of their class the signs, so that all the class can use this medium for communication. In our experience, even young children are very excited about signing and indeed very good at learning this type of skill. The effect of all the children being able to sign to the deaf child is that they are no longer isolated. Signing can become just another common language in the classroom. Now you really can ask the children to be very quiet !

Signing can begin in a very simple way, even if there are no children at present in the class who use signing. Figure 1:4 shows some simple signs, common to many signing systems, which can allow children to introduce themselves to each other. Children can use these simple signs to begin to sign their name, in a sentence, as an answer to a question. They can also sign their address. This could be part of work on maps in geography (see chapter five).

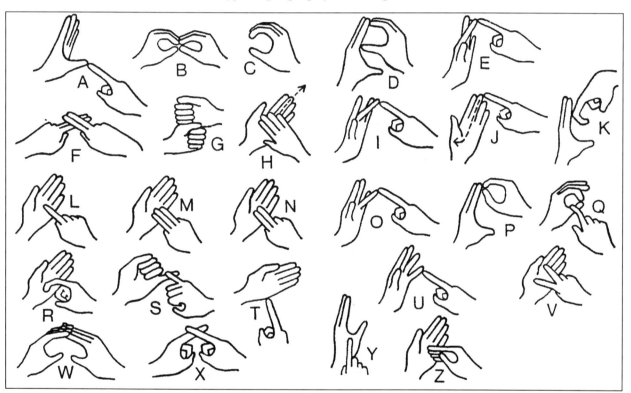

Figure 1:3 The Standard Manual Alphabet

The children can develop their skills by using one of the published sign systems such as Makaton, which is available from The National Society for Mentally Handicapped Children, Pembridge Hall, 17 Pembridge Square, London W2 4EP. Alternatively, they can make up their own 'mime' signs. You will find that children's mime will be very close to the real 'signs' and can convey meaning to children who sign, even if they are not exactly the same signs. Giving non-signing children the confidence to communicate with signing peers will help both groups of children to integrate with each other.

The whole class as peer tutors

Peer tutoring for the authors is children teaching children within their own class. This needs no school-wide reorganisation or indeed whole-school policy (an oft used excuse for inaction). This does not mean that if you put children together then you are implementing a peer tutoring system. What this approach to peer tutoring does need is a careful skills training programme, so that children learn how to teach one another well.

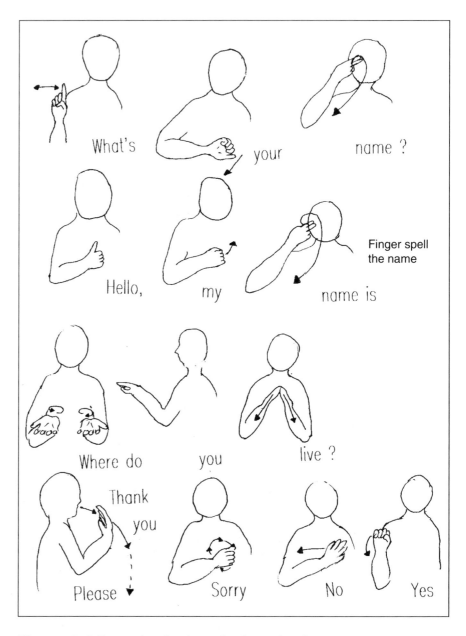

Figure 1:4 Some basic signs for introductions

16

For children with special needs, not only does this system have the advantage of giving the children support every minute of the day, as opposed to when the support teacher is available, but it also increases the number of other children with whom the child forms relationships, reducing feelings of exclusion and isolation. As a child's peer group continue together up through the school and sometimes on to other phases, the tutoring relationships can continue to support children, long after they leave the class in which they were established.

We noted earlier the way in which peer feedback forms and influences the self-esteem of children. Peer tutoring is an excellent way to increase children's experience of receiving positive feedback from their peers, both for learning successes and for using helpful behaviours.

The differentiated curriculum

Whilst it is recognised by teachers that it is good practice to match the task to the ability of the children and their present level of attainment, many teachers feel daunted by the enormity of such a task. The solution has been ability grouping within classes to enable the teacher to produce work of a suitable level for each group of children. There are inherent problems in this way of dealing with differentiation.

Children performing at a high level in reading might be presumed to be good mathematicians as well; poor readers might find they are assessed as very poor scientists. This was certainly found to be the case during the first years of the Key Stage 1 Assessments. Lawton (SEAC Key Stage 1 SATs Training Conference, 1990) found that children were wrongly assessed by teachers as having poor maths and science skills because they were poor readers. The SAT assessments established that the children were at a much higher level in their understanding than their teachers had assessed. It seems that the children's failure as readers had established them as 'low ability' in all curriculum areas in the teacher's perception. The feedback that children receive when this happens has implications for their self-esteem.

It is extremely time consuming for any teacher to devise work designed for many different levels of skill and literacy. Even when great care is taken by conscientious teachers to match tasks to levels there can never be a perfect match, not even if every child is given specially devised work. This is because no teacher can ever be a perfect assessor of a child's ability. At best they can only get a partial match, as the whole issue of children's learning is too complex for anything more. The best possible people to assess their own understanding, their competence and the level of skills required by tasks are the children themselves. The children will not do what they cannot do. They will attempt things just a little outside their present range and take those small risks. In order for children to have the freedom to use their own judgement teachers need to begin offering children open-ended tasks that allow wide interpretation.

One of the things that conscientious teachers often find when they try to put individualised teaching or differentiated approaches into action is that it is incredibly time consuming. Indeed, when interviewed, teachers expressed their concern over integrating children with special needs because they felt guilty at the amount of time spent preparing specialised work for just one child. The same view is held of children who don't 'behave'.

It may also be felt that this individualised approach is necessary to meet the needs of up to a third of the children in a class, not just the few who are statemented. When faced with these feelings of guilt teachers want support in the classroom in order to manage this workload. In order to support the third of the class deemed to need individual help teachers would need to have upwards of ten support teachers or ancillaries in their classroom. This is often exactly what teachers say. Teacher perceptions of the lack of this sort of people resource leads to feelings of frustration and anger, and may well be the reason for some teachers wanting children with special needs to be withdrawn from the classroom or the school and placed in a 'special' setting.

One of the difficulties inherent in this individualised teaching approach where the teacher provides carefully graded work for each child, often in the form of worksheets, is that it leads to dependency by the child on the teacher's preparation. The more dependent the child gets, the harder the teacher must work to keep that child interested and supplied with appropriate work. The more work is prepared by the teacher, the more dependent the child gets upon the teacher's judgement of what they need to do next.

There is an alternative way of dealing with this which allows the children to take far more responsibility for themselves, whilst still catering for the needs of all those in the class. As an example, a teacher of our acquaintance was regularly preparing worksheets for several children in her class with reading difficulties. The sheets used cloze procedure and hand drawn pictures to encourage the children to read the book by finding the missing words. An alternative is to give all the children in the class different books and ask each of them to design a worksheet that had missing words, questions about what happened and pictures to help make it interesting. This is easy for the poorer readers as it is copying work, and can also be quite challenging for the more able children. When these are complete the children can swop and answer each other's worksheets. They can even do the marking!

This approach can be applied to shared reading. A group of children in one class came back from reading to the infants asking if they could do a puppet show, because the children weren't very good at listening to stories. The story they devised was based upon the sound of the week, utilising a phonic technique. It seems as if children with special needs who have low self-esteem are so busy protecting their self image as reading failures that they are unable to make use of techniques such as phonics, when offered in the 'dependent' setting of support teacher and child. But when they are in the role of teacher they can use these techniques to help others. In so doing they explore and learn the phonics themselves.

A different role for the teacher

Clearly the difference for the teacher's workload when the children are devising their own worksheets is considerable. It is our belief that when teachers are doing 80 per cent of the work, through preparation, and the children 20 per cent through the activity, the possible learning is only 20 per cent of the potential for that piece of curriculum and the workload for the teacher is unreasonable.

A rule of thumb is to check out any planned activity for the 20 per cent to 80 per cent rule. A teacher, working on electricity, was crumbling under the workload created by a vertically grouped, mixed ability class who were not being responsive to her carefully-produced worksheets. A different approach was suggested. Initially, the children were asked to make a light bulb light up in the most interesting way they could. They were put in groups and given ten 'cubes' to spend in the teacher's electricity shop. Each item of hardware had a different price in cubes. They had to plan and negotiate and pay for the equipment they needed, try it out, evaluate the circuit, swap equipment and make it better. The teacher's involvement remained as the provider of equipment, not the fount of all knowledge. The children were not asked to write but to plan, think, evaluate and work together. At the end of the lesson, each group showed their circuit and explained what they had done and how they had done it. In this way not only do they learn about their own circuit by doing, but about several others by watching and listening. They are also engaged fully in the process and do not switch off.

This way of turning around the 20/80 balance means a changing role for the teacher. The onus is not on the teacher to be super prepared and to know everything. The preparation becomes the structuring of the learning experience to ensure maximum participation, involvement and responsibility by all the children. The role of the teacher is changed from that of 'teaching' to that of 'providing an environment' in which children can learn.

The more responsibility children are given, the more independent they can become. Independent children allow teaching to become the relaxed and satisfying experience that most teachers imagined it might be when they began their careers.

It is understandable that many teachers have become preoccupied and anxious about their own performance as a teacher, with the assumption that if you teach something well then the children must be learning. When the children fail to learn, the natural conclusion is that there is something wrong with the children. It is much harder to stand back and become a reflective teacher who starts to think about the children's learning and when children fail, asks 'What have I missed out?', 'What do they need now?', 'How can I restructure the task?' .

Assessment

With this changing role comes the opportunity to be an observer of children's learning in the classroom. Observing children during their task is the best possible way of assessing their present understanding. Usually this is a rushed and ad hoc affair in the primary classroom. By using the structures suggested in the book assessment can become a key part of the teaching process. It can enable the teacher to plan the next activity to meet the children's needs as observed. One of the skills the teacher needs to acquire is the ability to detect, from their observations, the group and interpersonal skills that the children need in order to gain the maximum they can from the curriculum being offered.

Teachers will still need to devise worksheets but these begin to relate far more to the skills for learning, e.g. group work, asking questions, listening (see examples in chapter three). These worksheets are often based upon children's observations of each other or provide a format to allow reflection after a lesson, rather than content and information.

The practice that the children have in reflecting on their performance in a group enables them to develop their skills in group work. The children are then better able to meet the criteria for successful participation in groups outlined in National Curriculum technology, science, maths, English, history, geography, and P.E. As the children practise and improve their skills at working together the opportunities for the teachers to observe and assess children in groups increase, cutting down the problems associated with the volume of teacher assessments to be made.

Using the 80/20 rule children become experienced at planning their work, organising themselves, observing each other and reflecting on their own learning. It then becomes possible to teach them the skills of self-assessment, peer assessment and recording progress. Since the introduction of the National Curriculum the cry from teachers has been 'Where do I find the time to do all this assessment and recording?'. The answer is to teach the children how to make effective and accurate assessments themselves so that your role is one of moderator.

An important aspect of this is to share the criteria of the assessment with the children. Even young children and those with special needs can understand what they need to be able to do to 'get good marks'. In our view it is good teaching practice to be able to state the criteria for success in 'child speak' so that the children can understand what they need to do. Changing the National Curriculum criteria into child speak is an effective way of coming to terms with what it means for the teachers themselves.

Working in this way means that an important role of the teacher in carrying out their obligation to make assessments against the National Curriculum criteria can be accomplished with less stress to the teacher and the students.

CHAPTER 2

Changes in Teaching Style

In order to get the best from this programme we have found that certain classroom control techniques and discipline approaches work better than others. This might mean teachers changing their own behaviour and letting go of practices which have appeared to serve them adequately so far. We do not underestimate the difficulty in changing one's own behaviour; lapses are inevitable at first — and forgivable!

Waiting

Waiting out the talk and the chatter in order to get silence so that you can talk seems to be effective. This is hard at first but if you are persistent it means that in the end the children come to take responsibility for their own noise and it is a quicker, more effective method than shushing and shouting or 'hands on heads'. The authors have been known to sit out the noise, waiting patiently for up to half an hour with particularly difficult groups. This is only necessary the first few times!

'I' Statements

Using 'I' language for 'upsets' is a technique promoted by Thomas Gordan (1974). The essential part of this approach is to eradicate 'you' statements. A teacher happening upon a spill might well say, 'Now look what you've done, Jamie, you really are clumsy.' 'I' language would replace this with a statement that tells the child exactly what behaviour has upset you, and how that behaviour affects you. This might change what you say to something like 'Jamie, when you knock the water over after I've asked you to be careful I feel really upset because the water has gone over the other paintings and it could have been avoided if you had done as I asked.'

In our experience this method of dealing with upsets has an enormously positive effect when used over a period of time. We feel that this is because the feedback in terms of specific behaviour allows students to maintain or recreate a positive view of themselves. It allows them to think 'I am an OK person who tends to knock things over', as opposed to the all-pervading and damaging 'I am clumsy'. In addition it presents a model of dealing with upsetting incidents which the pupils can copy when they get upset. If the students have seen and heard you speak in this way they are able to try similar language themselves. Having been a part of an exchange which deals with an upset in a constructive way, allows students to deal with each other's negative feelings in a positive way instead of the more destructive name calling and hitting or lashing out. Finally, using such 'I' language means that neither party gets cross or angry and the positive environment in the classroom is fostered and maintained.

Broken records

Using the 'broken record technique' rather than a confrontation approach is very effective in the classroom. An example might be a request for a child to put a prohibited toy or game away rather than demanding with threats. A very difficult child might well refuse such a request. A teacher using the broken record technique would say: 'David, I want you to put that computer game in my drawer otherwise it will get broken.' Upon the reply 'Don't want to,' or similar, the teacher can acknowledge his reluctance but repeat the request, perhaps saying 'I know you would rather keep the game but I want you to put it in my drawer, please, otherwise it might get broken.' The technique is to listen to each excuse or outburst and acknowledge what has been said by the child but finish by repeating calmly what you want the child to do. It may be that you do this without a break or you may continue to deal with other children and keep coming back to the difficult child with the same acknowledgement of their view and then your repeated request.

It is our experience that even the most difficult child will calm down and eventually say, 'I think I'll put this in miss's drawer otherwise it might get broken'. The child has ownership of the decision to put the toy in the desk and a habit of complying to calm requests has been initiated. There are alternatives of which all teachers will already be aware. For instance, 'David! Put that computer game in my drawer, at once! David, if you don't do as I say I'll send you to Mrs James!' This may or may not allow the teacher to win, but it will be a temporary victory. Again, the modelling for the other children in the class is powerful. Using the technique outlined shows them that there are ways of getting what they want without resorting to threats and violence.

Modelling is useful, but the effectiveness of these techniques can be further enhanced by teaching them to the children. Both these methods ('I' language and broken record) can be explicitly taught to the children in the same way as the other skills outlined in this book are taught. If the children are taught these techniques following a period of time when their teacher has been using this approach they will recognise and pick up the skill much more quickly.

Using open questions about feelings

Using open questions and asking children how they feel is a valuable approach, particularly when there is a student-to-student upset. Teachers can acquire the habit of saying to one of the pupils 'OK, so what happened here?' and then to the other 'Is that what you think ? Tell me what you think happened here.' Ensure that the rule is established that they do not interrupt each other's account of the incident. This establishes the fact that both parties will have a chance to say what they think and their teacher will not jump to conclusions. This method is far more effective than a teacher saying, 'You again Mark. Well I might have known there would be trouble with you around.' Having listened to both sides, it is effective to get into the habit of asking them how they feel after they have explained what happened, because that is often the key to the whole incident. Only after this should any attempt at judgement be made by the teacher, although talking it through is often enough to calm the situation down.

As the children get used to their teacher dealing with incidents in this way the teacher and class may progress to the class court. This is far more effective than any decision made by a teacher. If circumstances allow, a 'class jury of peers' can be asked what they feel about the incident after the children have described their point of view. Again, no interruptions should be allowed whatever is being said, as long as all are allowed their turn. The children can be asked to decide what would be a fair way of dealing with the situation. One thing children are incredibly good at is knowing what is fair! It is often teachers who get that aspect of classroom justice very wrong.

Processing the learning

Another strategy which helps teachers to run this programme most effectively is to remember to process *everything* you do with the children. It is a little like immediate marking of children's work. Processing means that you ask them at the end of every single exercise how well they thought they did and how well others in their group did. This allows children to realise that they have learnt something and that they have succeeded. This verbal affirmation of success, not by the teacher but through the voices of themselves and their peers is a most powerful way to change a negative self-image and low self-esteem into one which is positive.

Creativity as an approach

Creativity is not here linked with the story telling in English or with drawing in art. It allows children to be creative and suggest solutions and strategies themselves.

Encouraging creativity, brain-storming and problem-solving

approaches can have surprisingly positive results. A class of year 5 children, asked to brain-storm a topic on time, planned a whole section of their topic around the physical decay of different material used in car manufacture when subjected to oil, salt, vinegar and water and the relative depreciation in monetary value of cars of different types. Far more enterprising and relevant than watching the bread and fruit decay, which was the teacher's perception of their interest and level!

Celebrating success

Creating opportunities for success and going 'over the top' when it is achieved is a very good way of turning round unsuccessful children and giving them a different view of what success in school can mean and feel like. The authors have used computer graphics extensively to create certificates and congratulations sheets to celebrate non-academic and then academic achievements. P.E. is a good place to begin. Art awards, 'good ideas' certificates, golden books for recording tidy or organised behaviour, public commendations of helpfulness can all help to give tastes of success to children who have no experience of how to deal with success in school. Academic achievement usually has success awards built in but teachers can invent celebrations for all children which publicly acknowledge hard work and effort as well as ability.

One class were re-motivated into swimming through the use of home-produced certificates. The school could not afford to finance the 'real' ones and the children could not afford the official 'badges' that had previously been available. Children who were good swimmers had become unmotivated because the lessons seemed to be just practice with no visible reward for improvements. In addition the children's previous teacher had tried to discipline and motivate them by using removal of privilege for not working hard enough. One such privilege was being 'allowed' to go swimming. Previously used as a negative influence on the children, swimming was transformed into a positive influence. The advantage of home grown certificates is that they can be personalised for the school, the class, the pool, the child and very importantly, the distance and stroke the swimmer used. All these aspects help children to assimilate their success as their own, as it is unlike anybody else's. Awarding the certificates in the classroom proved to be effective, as did awarding them in a full school assembly.

Teacher praise

Praise is a very powerful tool for the teacher to use. Praise and reward — especially in the children's own language such as ace, wicked and brill (or whatever terms are current) — provides statements which are often just as treasured as compliments that teachers make in their own phrases. Using praise to reinforce the behaviour that is wanted is effective in ensuring that behaviour is repeated. In order to maximise the effect of praise teachers can praise the children if they themselves praise someone's behaviour or work. If the teacher reinforces the children using praise to each other then the effect of teacher praise is multiplied. It can also ensure that all the children know which behaviours are desired by that teacher. Praise from the teacher and pupils for being independent, for helping others, for asking for help from one another will support a co-operative ethos within the classroom, which is extremely important for children with special needs to flourish.

Research has shown that being specific about what it is you are praising is far more effective than global statements. To say 'That shading is really very good in your picture' is far more effective at raising the children's awareness of success and thus their self-esteem than 'That is a good drawing'. As outlined above, children with low self-esteem and failure attribution have a problem hearing good things about themselves. For these children it is even more important to use specific praise to break the negative attribution cycle.

Trying to eradicate sarcasm, 'showing up' and 'put downs' from their own vocabulary is important for teachers if they are to foster the positive regime in which children with special needs will flourish. It will be necessary to challenge put downs made by children in the classroom. A useful mechanism which works towards a healthy self-esteem for all pupils is to impose a 'punishment' of the child giving two 'put ups' (or compliments) for every 'put down'.

CHAPTER 3

Skills Training and the Curriculum

Teaching these skills first

We agree with Alexander (1992) that group work needs careful planning if it is to be effective and children are to remain on task. We maintain that children also need to be deliberately taught the skills that they need to do this. It is our view that while whole class teaching has its place, the failure of group work in schools that has been observed by H.M.I. and Alexander should not be abandoned for whole class teaching but replaced by the effective group work that can be achieved by skills based teaching.

It is our belief that children do not want to be naughty or lazy or aggressive but that often that is all that they know. What this book does is to provide a programme of skills training which allows children to change these behaviours based upon a model provided by the teacher and numerous opportunities to practise their new skills. It is also a programme that offers a way of delivering the curriculum to a diverse group and allows classroom teachers to include children of all abilities and those children with special needs in the same curriculum. To that extent it is a pedagogy.

What skills should we reach?

The authors believe that we need to teach children the following skills:

• how to listen to each other and to value each other;

• how to talk about their feelings, including their anxieties, so that they can hear that others have the same anxieties as them, and that jointly they can work out ways of overcoming these anxieties. In this way they can become known to one another and trust can be built up.

• how to give feedback on success to their peers so that they can receive realistic positive feedback from their peers;

• how to ask for help;

• how to give help and to become effective and competent tutors, including using a small steps approach, giving praise and verbal rewards;

• how to work co-operatively, through finding out and maximising each others' strengths, target setting on skill areas where they are less strong then practising those in the co-operative group setting;

• how to reflect on what they have learnt, processing their own and others' performances and contributions in a group;

• how to self-organise and take responsibility, both as an individual and as a group member

Teaching these skills first

Some teachers who have tried to combine process skills and curriculum content give up because they object that the children find this way of doing it too babyish or they won't or can't work together saying for example that their partner is 'too slow' and 'messes it up'. Teachers who have worked in the way outlined within this book have found that if you share with the children the reasons why they are doing the activity in this way then they see the learning on two levels. They became aware of their own skills, through the process, and the curriculum, through the content.

In this skills training, it is often only necessary to draw children's attention to what it is that you want them to do, give them a chance to practise it and then reinforce it through observation, assessment and feedback. In the examples outlined below there are suggestions as to what you might say to children to raise their awareness; what activity might give them an opportunity to experience or practise a skill; and structures which would allow children to learn a part of the National Curriculum whilst giving an opportunity to assess both the content and the skills.

In order to improve children's effectiveness in any skill, teachers need to look at the outcome that is desired and break that down into manageable steps for the children. This is the case whether the skill is reading and writing, multiplication and division, speaking and listening or being helpful and supportive. Teachers will need to teach the children a skill within a very structured context, after which they can give the children the chance to practise the skill in a variety of contexts.

We believe that the most effective way of teaching the skills necessary for including children with special needs follows this pattern. The skills of listening and speaking, asking for and giving help need to be taught deliberately through structured activities. However, these skills should not then remain in that context. The teacher should offer the opportunity for the children to use the skills they have learned within the context of the curriculum delivery. This maximises the ability of the children to transfer their inclusion skills into their normal behaviour. In this book we illustrate the way in which teachers can teach the skills of inclusion for children with special needs to both the special and the mainstream children. We also give examples of the way in which this can be used in the curriculum delivery.

It is clear from the contents of this book that we feel that the beginning of inclusion for children with special needs is the improvement of the communication skills of all the children in the classroom. Those who are receiving the children who are perceived as 'different' or 'difficult' need to be able to communicate effectively with the incoming children. They need to know what to do to make them feel welcome and supported but not patronised. The children with special needs likewise need to be able to communicate with their peer group in order to ensure acceptance and inclusion. This is vitally important because the children need to work against the perceptions and prejudices of their very difference.

This book therefore begins with the skills of communication, that are so vital to the relationships between the members of any group. These skills are identified and broken down into small steps which can be taught to all the children in a class. The way in which we have broken down these communication skills might be seen as a starting point for all teachers, whether mainstream or special needs, primary or secondary. It is not claimed as the only way or the most exhaustive. It is recognised that other types of division are possible and might be appropriate with certain age ranges and specific difficulties. Teachers will no doubt use their own particular knowledge of their children to tailor the size of divisions and teaching steps to their particular needs.

Combining skills training with curriculum content

The following chapters in this book are organised in the way outlined below. The communication skill being addressed and the skills breakdown is outlined alongside the illustrative activities which could be undertaken. These are linked with a curriculum area and a specific difficulty that a child might have. These can be adapted to use with different age groups.

The activities in this book are just a selection of those that have been used and proved to be successful at raising children's awareness of the skills involved in being part of an integrated classroom. The activities give the children the opportunity to learn those skills through, rather than at the expense of, time spent on the curriculum.

Initially it may be appropriate to teach a particular skill in the context of the skill itself. This means that children are able to concentrate on the skill and begin to understand what it is and how it can be used. However the further practice of that skill needs to be set in the curriculum. There are two reasons for this. First, the demands of the curriculum are such that the children would not have time to practise the skill as well as working on the curriculum area. Second, the skills are more readily transferred and used in the classroom if they are seen to be part of the way in which the curriculum is delivered in that classroom. This transference into all of the curriculum is the factor which teachers with whom we have worked have said is the most influential in changing the nature of the classroom, the children and their workload.

For this reason you will find that some activities, particularly those which initiate a skill, are not set in a special needs or curriculum context. However, many of the activities are set in a very specific context of the National Curriculum and in the context of children with a particular special need, as well as the skill that is being addressed. The activities that have this three layered approach are indicated as follows.

Activity

Special needs context........................
National Curriculum area........................
Skill............................

These activities are meant as an illustration, not as a blueprint for the only way in which the skill could or should be taught. From the illustrations given we would hope that teachers could transfer the way in which the skill and curriculum content can work together into their own particular context. This might mean looking quite carefully at the way in which the curriculum is currently being delivered in the classroom and re-thinking that delivery to ensure that the skills necessary for the inclusion of children with special needs are being taught to all the children in the class.

This book and its activities is not intended only for those who have children with specific special needs in their classroom. All our classrooms have children of widely different abilities, backgrounds and maturity. This is true even of the most homogeneous group of children. The skills needed to ensure that children who are clearly different are included into the mainstream classes are relevant to all children. A classroom where children are able to communicate with each other, express their feelings, ask for help, offer support and teach each other, is one where children experience positive relationships with their peers. In such a classroom time spent on sorting out interpersonal disputes is at a minimum, allowing the teacher to ensure that his or her energies are engaged in the teaching and learning process.

Guide to using the activities

Chapter 4 : Non-verbal communication

Special needs context - visually impaired ✴
Curriculum content - mathematics and English ✴
Skills breakdown

- body posture: facing the other person; forward leaning; appropriate distance

- facial expression: interested expression; head nods; empathy

- eye contact: appropriate amount

Chapter 5 : Initial verbal skills

> **Special needs context** - speech and language disorders
> **National Curriculum content** - geography
> **Skills breakdown**

• parroting: repeating back what you have heard using the same words

• summarising: repeating back the main points

• paraphrasing: interjecting summaries to check out the meaning and understanding

• combining and using: using the skills to help the other person to talk more, to understand and to remember

Chapter 6 : Asking questions and giving information

> **Special needs context** - severe learning difficulties
> **National Curriculum content** - science, maths and English
> **Skills breakdown**

• identifying and using a wide variety of talk

• asking and answering questions: personal information; factual information

• open and closed questions: asking questions which help the other person to give the information

Chapter 7 : Research through interviewing

> **Special needs context** - emotional and behavioural difficulties
> **National Curriculum content** - history
> **Skills breakdown**

• asking questions: peer tutoring skills

• interviewing: asking open questions and using paraphrasing to help them to clarify

• researching and presenting information

> **Special needs context** - hearing impaired
> **National Curriculum content** - English
> **Skills breakdown**

- our feelings: talking about feelings

- disclosure and trust: sharing personal information and building up the trust needed between supportive peers; giving and receiving compliments

- asking for help: identification of personal needs; role playing asking for help

- giving feedback: recognising the helpfulness of others; feedback skills

The structures used in this book

Random pairs

When children are left to stay in friendship groups or pairs they may not get to know other members of the group. If this is allowed to continue the children will not trust one another and will not be prepared to talk openly about their feelings, fears, frustrations or ideas in a group. This in turn will interfere with the group's potential ability to complete a task. Also, if children are left in friendship pairs they assess, judge and comment on one another's performance on the basis of information gained from first impressions. In this way stereotypes are maintained rather than challenged.

The use of random pairs can ensure that students get to know one another and provide an opportunity for girls and boys, pupils of different ethnic backgrounds, and children with special educational needs to work together.

The methods outlined below provide a number of different ways of helping children to work with someone who is not their best friend. If these methods are used over and again and the reasons for using them are explained clearly to the children, they soon come to expect that they will work in this way, and in time may choose a partner based on appropriate needs for a given task. For example one child may say to another, 'I know you are good at drawing and I am not. Will you work with me for this?'

Pairs numbering

Number the children so that there are two of each number and instruct the children to find the person in the room with the same number as them. The same ends can be achieved using cards with numbers written on them, or coloured dots and cards, or symbols photocopied onto coloured papers.

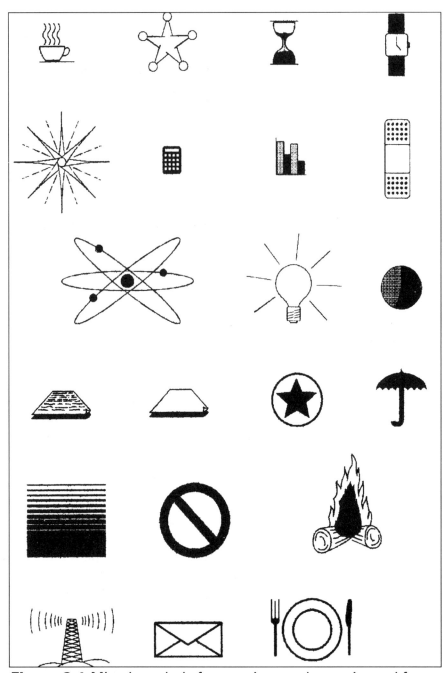

Figure 3:1 Mixed symbols for creating random pairs and fours

Matching pairs

Use cards (birthday, Christmas, Diwali, Eid, postcards, football cards) cut in half and placed in a bag. The children choose a card, then find the person with the other half of their card.

Opposites

For children who can read, the words of opposites can be used, if there are any who cannot read pictures or drawings can be used. These can be curriculum related or from other sources such as Meg and Mog, Temple and Pyramid, sun and rain, cloud and snow.

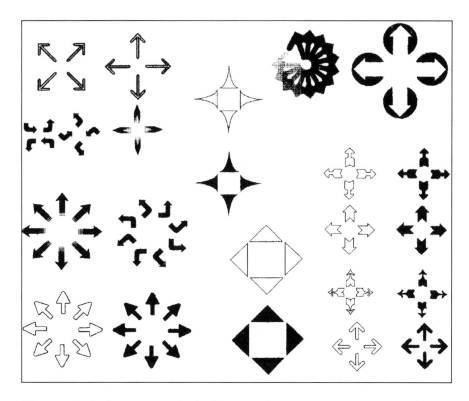

Figure 3:2 Arrow symbols for creating random pairs and fours

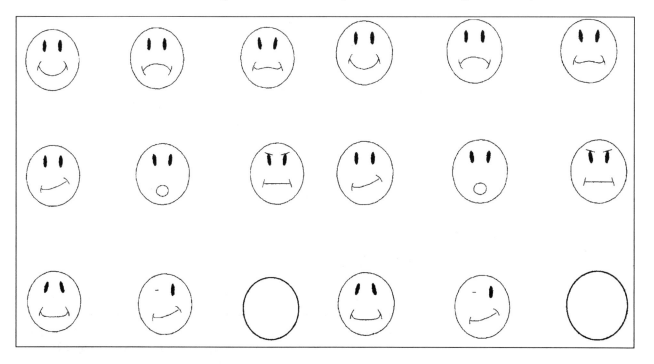

Figure 3:3 Faces for creating random pairs and fours

33

Random groups

The phrase 'get into groups' can be intimidating and frightening for some children, particularly the ones always left out or actually pushed out or rejected. Such experiences are damaging for children, and they may come to hate group work as a result.

The methods outlined below provide ways to divide the class randomly into groups of different sizes, whilst allowing children to feel more secure than when left to their own choosing. Working in this way children can learn about their other classmates and extend their friendships.

With all of these activities it is important that the teacher firmly but gently insists on this approach while maintaining a light atmosphere. Explaining clearly the reasons for working randomly helps, as does correct pacing i.e. little and often at first, gradually building up to a 'this is what we do here' approach.

The methods outlined above for random pairs can be adapted for groups i.e numbers; cards; letters of the alphabet; five aspects of Eygpt or the weather for groups of five; postcards, birthday cards etc. cut into fours or sixes.

Animals

Cards with the names of animals are given out, the children are told to make the noises of the animals on their card.

Birthdays

Ask the children to form groups based on similar birthdays, signs of the zodiac, height, position in the family, hobbies, etc.

Dash

The teacher calls out a number, e.g. twos, sixes, fours, and the children have to dash to the nearest people to form a group of that size.

Friendship groups

It is appropriate for children to work in their friendship groups sometimes. This is particularly important if you are focussing on a different skill, for example encouraging them to include or coax back into their group a child who has temper tantrums or runs off, or if you are introducing a new skill for the first time.

Jigsaw groups

This is a very effective technique for areas of the curriculum that require information exchange, for example history or geography. The children are assigned to groups of five or six (this can be done on a random or friendship basis). These may be known as home, base or topic groups. Each child is then allocated a theme within the topic, for example if the topic is Romans, one child in the group may be gladiator, one stone mason, one temple initiate, one household manager, one road builder, etc. Each child then joins a group of the same theme, so that all the household managers meet in one group, and carry out a task which enables them to increase their knowledge about that theme. The children then return to base or home groups and teach each other about the different themes they have developed. It is best if the home groups are given a task, e.g. teaching a younger age group or doing an assembly about the topic, so that there is a purpose to the information exchange.

Clearly this strategy requires some speaking, listening, reporting and interviewing skills. The way these might be taught is outlined in the sections on history, emotional and behavioural difficulties, and interviewing skills.

Circles

In this book we have acknowledged the difficulty many children and adults experience when talking in front of their peers in a large group, and we have accordingly recommended many techniques and strategies as alternatives to the whole group. It is our view, however, that children also need to be in the whole circle, and practise, through carefully planned structures, speaking and listening in the whole group. At first the children need to do this a little (perhaps no more than five minutes) and often (probably every day). After a while they will be able to sit in the circle without discomfort or unease for protracted periods.

For effective circle work it is best if some guide-lines are followed:

1. The children and the teacher should all be on the same level, either sitting on the floor or on chairs.
2. If on chairs, there should be no desks, so there is no barrier between the children and their peers.
3. It is also important that they form a true circle and not an oval or an amoeba, as a circle ensures that everyone has eye contact.

As well as helping children to get to know one another by using random pairs and groups where they can be encouraged to find out and then use one another's names, it is essential to give children structures to learn the names of everyone in the group. We have known children who after five years in the same class still did not know each other's names, they knew their friends' names or friends plus members of the same sex, but not others.

Name circle

This is a useful way to help them know one another's names.

Taking it in turns around the circle, each child says the first phrase (My name is ...) and then puts in their own ending. When everyone has introduced themselves a second phrase is used around the circle, and so on. For example:

1. *My name is ...*
2. *My name is ... and this is ...* (introduce next door neighbour)
3. *My name is ... .* (use an alliterative word to include a hobby or interest eg Swimming Susan, Roaming Richard, Football Fazal)
4. *My name is ... and I am good at/ like ...*

The first time this is used it is probably enough to do just the first phrase. The children will need to use the name exercises many times in order to help all of them learn all the names of all the others.

News/sharing circles

For children to gain further knowledge of each other and to practise both listening to each other and turn taking, a circle time where children share information about themselves is very useful.

As with the name circle the children complete the following sorts of sentences:

One thing I enjoyed doing this week ...
I feel happy when ...
What I like/dislike, about my brother/sister/ family is ...
When I have time to myself at home I like ...
One thing that makes me cross in this class is ...

The sentences can cover anything that seems relevant at the time but usually a certain amount of 'safe' personal information is necessary in order to build up trust and empathy in the group.

Ball roll for names and other sharing activities

Once the children have been in the circle with each other a few times and heard information about one another they can be encouraged to try this exercise which is one of recall and feedback.

A ball, beanbag or something similar is used. One child has the ball and says:

My name is ... and this is ... (saying the name of the child they roll the ball to).

They can gradually build up to saying

Swimming Susan who likes strawberry yogurt to footballer Fazal who hates spiders.

The rule is that they must roll the ball to a different person each time. This is a technique that helps children to value what has been said by others and teaches elements of friendship skills.

For some children the effect of hearing that they were heard encourages them to change their behaviour and they start to ask for circle time instead of disrupting it. As with all of these strategies teacher praise is a crucial part of developing and maintaining appropriate turn taking and listening behaviour. A statement like:

I am really proud of you for remembering that Jade doesn't like her name, Clinton. I thought that you were not listening and I was wrong!

has powerful effects on the children.

Compliments circles

Once the children have begun the process of giving feedback as outlined in the previous exercise, they can go on to develop this skill by playing the compliments game.

Ask the children to finish the phrase

I am the best person in the world at ...

They should go round the circle twice for this, as it helps to raise self-esteem. Repeat with the phrase:

I am not very good at ...

Then ask the children to tell the one next them something they are good at. The other child says thank you. This can be extended by getting the children to brain-storm all the ways people behave when they are being friendly. The teacher or the children then write these out on cards in the following way:

This person has a nice smile.
This person helps me out when I am in trouble.
This person has lovely eyes.
This person is good at listening.

There need to be about three times the number of cards as there are children in the group for this, although the same phrase can be used several times.

The cards are placed in a bag, the bag is passed round and the children take out a card each until all the cards have gone. They then take it in turns to read out what is on the card, give it to someone , and say why they are giving it to them, e.g.

This person is helpful, this is for you Jaya because you went and got a plaster for me when I scraped my knee yesterday.

We find that when we work with teachers they are reluctant to do this game themselves, but when they try it with children the children love it.

Learning circles

This is a way of finishing off a topic or piece of skills training. It may be a follow up to a self assessment sheet, it may pull together a lengthy two day jigsaw style project or it may be used on its own. The children take it in turns to go round the circle and share what they have learned. We find this exercise often achieves several things; sometimes the children do not realise how much they have learned until they voice it; it gives the teacher an idea of where the children are up to so they can plan the next stage; and information for individual and whole-group assessment on that topic is available.

Taking turns using props

Despite first using the pair and small group structures outlined in this book, some teachers still experience extreme difficulties when they come to do circle time. They find that either children dominate the circle and talk out of turn or there are some who will not say anything — or both of these sorts of behaviours.

In this situation a 'conch' or prop helps. You can use a pencil case, board rubber, child's toy or anything to hand; the rule is that only the one with the prop in their hands can speak, they can speak for as long as they hold on to it, and it gets passed around to each child in turn. Individual children can choose to pass by passing the conch on but they are always offered the chance to speak because the conch always comes their way.

Any toy, ball, book or other prop can be used in this way to ensure turn taking. Variations from simply passing the prop around the circle can be to pass it to a person who is indicating by holding up a finger; to pass it to someone who has not yet had a turn, or to place it in a central point where a person may choose to take up the prop and add their comment.

Carousel

This is another strategy that is useful for information exchange, and for getting to know the others in the class. The topic for discussion can be either the curriculum subject or personal information.

The children are asked to get into pairs, then decide who is A and who is B. The As take their chairs and form a circle with their chairs facing outwards, the Bs then go and sit opposite them. In this way they form an inner and outer circle or a wheel within a wheel. Each A and B pairing spends five minutes discussing a topic, perhaps taking it in turns. The As then stand up and all move one place to their left or their right. Then the new pairing continue the discussion. The process can be repeated until all the students return to their original places. It may be best to start the process with half the class in each group, i.e. eight in the outside group and eight in the inside group, and another carousel in another part of the room with another sixteen students.

Goldfish bowl

This is a strategy which allows for assessment and as such it makes an

The Group members were

The best things about our group were

The worst things about our group were

We need to get better at

Figure 3:4 A group review sheet

ideal training place for skills. Again the students are organised into pairs and sorted into A and B. The students are then instructed to form two circles. The As sit in a circle facing inwards, and are instructed to discuss something. The Bs sit outside the circle but in a place where they can see the faces of the As. They are not to contribute to the discussion but they are to observe their partners' contributions, behaviours and skills. They may be given an

Our Group

	🙂	🙁	😐
How good was our group at making decisions ?			
How well did we organise the different jobs ?			
How good was our group at including everybody ?			
How well did we listen to each other ?			
How well did we listen to our group co-ordinater ?			
How good was our co-ordinater at listening to what we said ?			

What did I do to help my group get the job done ?

_____

What did I do that didn't help my group to get the job done ?

_____

What did others do that helped the group ?

_____

What could our group have done better ?

_____

What could I have done better to help my group ?

_____

Figure 3:5 Group review sheet

observation schedule for a particular skill and asked to assess or rate or comment on that skill. They then give feedback to their partners on their performance. This strategy lends itself to smaller groups; you may want to divide the children and have two or three fishbowls in the room.

Observers or spotters

It is important to teach children to observe one another because it is the pre-requisite skill for giving effective feedback, for peer

Name	Skills Circuit - Personal Record					
	Week 1	**2**	**3**	**4**	**5**

	Week 1	2	3	4	5
Skipping How many times without stopping ?					
Football dribble How many goals in a minute ?					
Bench steps How many in a minute ?					
Unihoc How many complete circuits of the obstacle course in a minute ?					
Bean bag throw Score in 10 throws. Target 1 = 5, target 2 = 10, target 3 = 15					
Ball and bat bounce How many times without stopping ?					

Notes on improvements

Figure 3:6 P.E. skills circuit sheet

assessment and hence for self assessment. Observation teaches children to look for certain criteria. The way to help them with this task is to provide them with grids or observation checklists, initially devised and written by yourself and later on devised and written by the children for each other.

Children can act as observers or spotters in groups or when the others are working in pairs, or as a role in a trio; i.e. speaker, listener, observer. Each child should take a turn at each role.

Debrief

This skill is an essential part of the approach to groupwork as outlined in this book. It is essentially about processing; the teacher asks the children to talk about the feelings they had whilst they were doing the exercise, and to say how effective they were at achieving the task or carrying out a skill. The debrief may be carried out by all group members or both people in a pair, or it may comprise information or behaviours observed by the observer.

Weekly Diary

Date : Monday ....to Friday..................

Subject	Comment 😊	🙁	☹
Maths			
English			
Science			
Tech.			
History			
Geog			
Art			
P.E.			
Other			

Next week I am going to try to. _____

Figure 3:7 Weekly diary sheet with target setting

Self-assessment

Once the children get used to the skill of debriefing orally they can be introduced to written sheets or grids. The grids can ask the children to individually say how they thought their group performed, what their own role in that process was, or how well they personally performed on the task set.

Children who can self assess and target set are well on the way to independent learning and can make the assessment role of the teacher far less arduous. Indeed the teacher's role becomes more one of moderator.

The children will soon be able to complete review sheets. These can

Autumn Term Review Think about the things we have done this term. Complete the following statements for yourself. **This term the things I have most enjoyed have been....** **The reason(s) I have enjoyed these things is/are....** **The things I have least enjoyed have been....** **The reason(s) I have not liked these things is/are...**	Think about the people in the class that you have worked with this term. Draw a diagram to show who you work with best and who you are least able to work with. ┌─────────────────────────────┐ │ **People with whom I can work best/least.** │ │ │ │ │ │ │ │ │ └─────────────────────────────┘ Why do you think that you can work with these people but not with others ?
List the sorts of lessons that keep you interested and in which you work hard. List the lessons that you find boring and in which you find it hard to work.	Think about the things you have achieved this term. Complete the following statements. You may wish to write about more than one thing. **One thing I have learned this term is....** **One thing I have got better at this term is....** **One thing I have realised I need to get better at is...** **My target for next term is to....**

Figure 3:8 Termly review booklet, with prompt questions

range from the very simple keeping of a diary, daily or weekly, to the more complex review at the end of a term or year. Several kept in conjunction with each other can help children to reflect on their learning, understanding and appreciating their progress and target setting for the future.

For schools that operate a Record of Achievement these skills are very important. They help to answer the complaint from teachers of lack of time to keep these records properly.

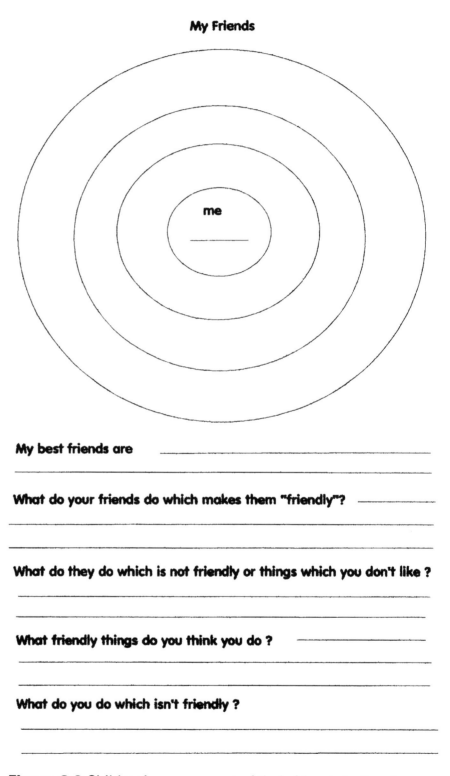

My Friends

me

My best friends are _____

_____

What do your friends do which makes them "friendly"? _____

_____

_____

What do they do which is not friendly or things which you don't like ?

_____

_____

What friendly things do you think you do ? _____

_____

_____

What do you do which isn't friendly ?

_____

_____

Figure 3:9 Children's assessment of their friends in the class

If children have made these sorts of records then they are far more able to assist the teacher in the ordering and keeping of relevant work and National Curriculum records as well as the other information on hobbies and interests more commonly entrusted to them.

The authors have evidence from many teachers with whom they have worked, that children who are taught through the structures and skills outlined here and in the rest of this book, will have a greater chance of being fully integrated into the mainstream classroom. Observation of the children's behaviour by the teacher will provide an assessment of the increased integration. Asking the children to map out their friends, as shown in figure 3:9 will provide another measure for the teacher. If this activity is carried out at the beginning and the end of a school year, the friendship and cooperative nature of the classroom will be shown through the increased proximity of the children in their drawings.

CHAPTER 4

Non-Verbal Communication

This chapter explores the non-verbal behaviours which help and hinder effective listening. Children with physical difference may find learning appropriate non-verbal behaviour quite difficult due to their physical condition. Children with no physical difference may make assumptions about those children with physical difference who 'look funny at me' because the former are reacting to non-verbal cues of which the latter are unaware. The former might in turn give out a message of dislike or disinterest through their own non-verbal behaviour. For both groups of students it is important that they are aware of the messages their bodies are giving, are able to recognise their own reactions to them and are given an opportunity to change those which are not helping them to communicate.

A very important aspect of non-verbal communication for children are signs which demonstrate that you are listening. This is important for helping children to look as if they are listening and concentrating on the teacher's talk. It is also vital if children are going to feel that they are listened to by each other. Many difficulties arise within classrooms because children talk to each other but rarely really listen to what other children are saying. Children whom we have taught, when watching a video of themselves at work in a group, recognised that the reason they could not get the job done was because 'everyone is talking and no one is listening !'

For children with special needs there might be many reasons why they have not been listened to. They may have problems speaking clearly, they might be regarded as having nothing important to contribute or they might have learnt that if you don't talk then you don't get ignored. For these children, knowing that you are being listened to, even through the non-verbal messages you receive, might be an important first step towards feeling part of a class or group.

The non-verbal behaviours which can affect both the ability to really listen and your appearance as a listener are eye contact, body posture and facial expression. It is easy to make children aware of these non-verbal signals and then help them to establish appropriate ones.

Body posture

The positioning and proximity of the body and its orientation and posture are important influences on the way that both speakers and listeners are perceived by others. For children with special needs it is helpful if they explore with their teachers and their peers the type of body position and posture with is most helpful for good communication. Children who lounge around or slump over their desks are likely to be perceived as uninterested and lazy. Children who are in the habit of sitting up and leaning slightly forward are more likely to be seen as interested and eager. Children can explore the way in which they read other people's body posture through structured experiences. They can try out the effect on their own feelings and on others' perceptions of them by experimenting and changing their own body posture. Children who are visually impaired can also join in this activity. Classmates can give them feedback about what is helpful to sighted children in terms of body posture by physically guiding them into the most useful postures.

Activity - Telling a story

Special needs context - visually impaired
Curriculum content - English AT 1, AT 3: Telling a story
Skill area - non-verbal communication

Ask the children to sit in threes and label them A, B and C. Ask A to talk to B about what they have been doing for the past week. Stop them after a couple of minutes and ask B to look as uninterested as

Figure 4:1 Children working in threes

they can. Stop the children after a couple of minutes and ask B to change their 'look' to one of great interest. C is an onlooker, observer or spotter. Their role is to notice what happens to the body posture of both A and B. After just five or six minutes stop the conversation and allow each child in the trio to tell the other two what they felt like, what they noticed about their concentration and ability to talk and listen and what they observed happening to their body posture. This debrief is very important in allowing children to become more aware of the effect of their body posture.

Facial expressions and head nods

The activity above can be repeated with any other topic of conversation. It could be a personal account of events or feelings, the re-telling of a familiar story, a recalling of information supplied in an earlier lesson by a television programme or a worksheet or provided by the teacher. It can be repeated to explore other important aspects of good listening such as facial expression and head nods.

It is likely that the children who were spotters in the above activity will have noticed that when children were looking interested they both leaned slightly forward, they faced each other, they had an interested expression on their face, they looked at the other person and they nodded in agreement and encouraged by saying 'mmmm' and 'yes' etc. Children who are visually impaired might need some time to try out different facial expressions and have their partners give them feedback. It would be unusual for this type of feedback to be given by peers, constructively, unless built into this type of structure. What visually impaired children might like to explore within this activity is the tone and expression created by the voice. The children can be asked to notice what happens to the tone and expression of the speakers' voices throughout this activity. This means that even blind children can be observers!

Activity - A story with 'feelings'

Special needs context - visually impaired
Curriculum content - English AT 1 and AT 3
Skill area - Using facial expression

Ask the children in their triads to change roles so that A is an observer, B is the speaker and C the listener. B is to retell a very familiar story and C is to listen. C is to try making their face look bored and uninterested. After a time ask them to alter their expression to one of interest and encouragement. A is to then feed back to the others what they noticed about what happened to the rest of their body posture. B and C can share how it felt as both listeners and speakers to have helpful facial expression and unhelpful expression.

In their groups of three, they again swap roles so that C is the

Spotter's Check Sheet

Name	Leaning Forward	Sitting face to face	Nodding / Smiling	Talking	Other
A					
B					

Figure 4:2 A spotter's check sheet

speaker, A the listener and B the observer. C is to talk about a time when they were very happy or sad. A is to listen and make their expression one which reflects the emotion of the story being told. After a couple of minutes ask A to change their expression to one which is the opposite of the emotion of the story being told. Again, ask the children to talk about what they noticed.

As a whole class, brainstorm the helpful listening behaviours and the unhelpful listening behaviours. Pin up this brainstorm of the two different behaviours in the classroom or ask the children to design a 'Rules sheet' or a poster to remind them about how to 'listen with your body'.

Eye contact

The appropriate use of eye contact is vital for speaking and listening. Some children who use inappropriate eye contact are seen to have learning difficulties, behavioural problems, poor concentration or poor listening skills. This appears to be because they don't look as if they are listening or interested so the teacher might assume uninterest

49

or lack of understanding. It may be that by not making eye contact whilst communicating the children find it more difficult to hear what is said and so understand. They might also find that it is more difficult to express themselves and be understood by others. Children need to explore the nature and effect of using different levels of eye contact in a structured setting so that they can use it more effectively in their day-to-day encounters. They might also appreciate the difficulties that visually impaired students have in hearing, even though their hearing is not impaired.

It is usually sufficient to draw students' attention to the importance of eye contact by taking them through exercises where they have none. Some party games such as 'Killer,' 'Wink' or 'Bunnies' are very useful just for getting children to make eye contact with their peers.

Activity - Number bonds

Special needs context - visually impaired
Curriculum content - maths AT 2 Number
Skill - eye contact

Tell the children:

Today, we are going to do are two things in maths. One is the sums and the other is to find out how important looking at someone is when you are working together. You must have heard teachers saying 'look at me when I'm talking to you'. I bet your mums say that too. When you were working together in your art groups the other day, Dale kept complaining that no one was taking any notice of him, didn't he? That was because no one was looking at him, only at what they were doing themselves. To do this we are going to work in pairs, but not with your friend. If you do, you might find that you look at them a lot because you know them very well and like them. It is sometimes more tricky to do that with someone you don't know yet.

I've got a bag here with shapes in it, which means that all of you, including the children who cannot see very well, can feel the shapes. To make it fair, I want all of you to shut your eyes. Feel the shape that you take out of the bag, then go up to other people. Open your eyes so you don't trip over — you're not as good at this as Suzanne and George. When you get to another person, close your eyes again and ask to feel their shape. If you have got the same shape then you are partners. Collect a pack of fuzzy felt, braille or ordinary number cards, whichever you need, and sit down together.

The cards available should have tactile spots, large numbers or braille numbers. For the braille cards there should be a print number for the sighted children as well as the braille number. Tactile spots can be useful for all the children. Ordinary playing cards can also be adapted and used.

The teacher continues:

Sit down with your partner and deal the cards. Now turn your chairs around so that you are back to back with your partner. One of you pick the first two of your cards and say them to your partner, as you try to add up the sum yourself. See if you and your partner get the same answer. If you don't then count the spots to check, (or use a calculator if the numbers are large).

Figure 4:4 Children working back to back

This activity can clearly be used to work on subtraction and multiplication and, with modified cards, division. It could be an activity which is built into the curriculum on a regular basis, even in those few minutes of dead time at the beginning and end of a session. Children can begin to make up the sums without using cards and adjust the level of questions to the expertise of their partner. Calculators used by the children in turn can make this activity fun and productive for all the children. Talking calculators for the blind can be used and enjoyed by sighted children as well as those who are visually impaired.

Ask the children to turn to face each other at the end of this activity and talk for three or four minutes about what they found difficult and what effect not being able to see each other had on the way they heard what was said. Ask them to talk about anything else that they noticed about working together without looking at each other. Ask three pairs to join together and share what it was that they found out about eye contact. Then as a whole class, one person from each group is to feed back to the whole class circle their group's feelings and findings.

Activity - Properties of shapes

Special needs context - visually impaired

Curriculum content - Maths AT4 Shape and Space

Skill - eye contact

The following day the children can try out the difference between having no eye contact and having good eye contact and explore its effect upon the way in which they hear and remember what is said.

Using the same method to get the children into random pairs, ask them to sit face to face, knee to knee. Give each pair a set of tactile shapes, either 2D flat plastic shapes or 3D shapes, depending on the age and level of the students. For a class with no blind students the tactile shapes can be substituted with a set of cards with shapes drawn on them. For those children who have some sight the cards will need to be large enough for them to distinguish the shapes. Children could have made these shape cards in a previous lesson, either by drawing them or using templates. The complexity of the shapes will depend on the ability of the children. Teachers might wish to have sets offering a variety of levels to allow for differentiation in classes with a wide variation of ability.

Introduce the activity:

One of you is going to look at or feel a shape and your job is going to be to describe that shape to your partner. You must try very hard to look at your partner as you talk to them, not at the shape. Your partner will not be able to see the shape so your description must be very clear. Tell them about the size, the number of sides and corners, the angles at the corners. You should not use the name of the shape.

If you are listening, you can try to guess the name of the shape or draw what you think it is. Look at your partner's face to help you to know how 'hot' you are. When you have both had a turn, put all your shapes together and make a picture using these shapes. You can use each shape up to three times (if you need to cut out more shapes you may) but you must use all the shapes at least once.

This allows children having described the shapes, to use them, see what their properties might actually be useful for and practise using the proper names of the shapes, as appropriate. They are offered peer support throughout this activity. Children with visual impairment can join in equally because they will be using tactile shapes and drawing around them or sticking them on with instant glue, but they will receive peer support for activities which might be difficult and would normally require a support teacher or ancillary, e.g. for cutting out shapes and placing them.

The activity is also co-operative in its structure so those children with special needs are not set up for failure. They are not put into the position of taking sole responsibility for knowing the names of the shapes. The responsibility for getting the answer is shared between the 'describer' and the 'guesser'. This reduces the chances of feeling a failure whilst not diminishing the feelings of success, an important aspect of this structure for all children with special needs and a low self-esteem.

After you have finished your picture I want you to join with another pair and describe your picture to them. Take it in turns so that each of you gives just one piece of information about the picture. The other pair try to draw or guess what the picture is of. When you have guessed, change over and the second pair can describe their picture.

As a whole class circle talk about the difference between working without eye contact and working with eye contact. Draw attention to the children who have difficulty with their vision and ask for their comments on difficulties in hearing and concentrating because of their visual impairment. Encourage the children to ask what would help them to know when they were being spoken to etc. Point out the skills that these children have in listening attentively and describing using words because they have little or no eyesight to help them.

CHAPTER 5

Initial Verbal Skills

Just as children need to become aware of the different aspects of non-verbal communication and be given the opportunities to practise the skills of non-verbal communication one at a time, so the same is true of verbal communication.

Each skill needs to be:

• broken into sub-skills;

• introduced in a situation where the children can talk about something personal to them;

• practised within a National Curriculum context;

• assessed in a variety of ways.

For children with special needs the advantage of going through these skills with all their classmates, in a structured, carefully graded way is that:

• they have an opportunity to excel in skills which are different to the ones they often struggle with, namely reading and writing;

• they experience the positive benefits of a peer being interested in them;

• they don't have to fight to be heard, which means they will not have to learn either disruptive behaviours to have a role now or assertiveness or advocacy skills later on.

Taking turns

Turn taking is hard for us all, children and adults alike, as any staff meeting will demonstrate. To begin to take turns at speaking and listening in the way the paired activities in this book stress is also excellent practice for those who do not have special needs:

• they learn to work with someone who may appear a little different from them;

• they learn that someone who looks or talks a little differently from them may actually have similar likes and dislikes, interests and hobbies;

• they widen their tolerance and improve their skills of inclusion.

It takes time to learn skills. At first the amount of time needed to establish or teach the skill and the number of opportunities for practice needed so that every single child in the class becomes proficient may seem frustratingly high. It is quite usual for teachers to feel anxious about the pace in relation to the content side of the National Curriculum. However having worked with a large number of teachers we have found that the time needed for teaching the skills gradually diminishes as the children become used to working in this way, and as they build up their skills.

Additionally the children become more able to take responsibility for their own organisation and recording, and gradually for peer and self assessment, so more time becomes available for actual teaching.

Many teachers are also delighted to find other benefits such as reduced stress levels as the children start to become less teacher-dependent for help, guidance and discipline.

Speech and language disorders and self-esteem

Of all the different types of special need it is those children with speech disorders who need the most practice in speaking and therefore who need others who have the skills to listen in an encouraging and empathetic way. It is also likely that children with speech disorders will benefit greatly from learning appropriate listening skills, and being in the position of teacher or helper.

In chapter one we noted:

• the importance of self-esteem for children with special needs;

• the high correlation between low self-esteem and poor academic achievement;

• the benefits of peer-tutoring for raising academic self-esteem.

For children with speech disorders speaking will always be an effort. They will continue to need special practice on specific aspects of language. Finding the time to give children with speech and language disorders such practice is often difficult for the busy classroom teacher and may leave the teacher feeling that they cannot meet the needs of the language disordered child in the mainstream classroom.

The advantages of using the structured programmes on verbal skills as described in this and the following chapters are:

• All the children are following the same programme so that the child with speech and language disorder knows that he/she is the same as the rest.

• Some of these structures may be the very ones prescribed by the speech therapists.

• If not, they may well lend themselves to specific adaptation in consultation with the speech therapist.

• The children who do not have a speech and language disorder have some skills to carry out the work that a speech therapist, class teacher or special needs support teacher would perhaps in other circumstances do. This means that the child with speech and language disorders can get lots of practice without being singled out as being different because they are working with an adult instead of a peer.

• The children who do not have a speech and language disorder get practice at revising their own ideas on a subject having listened carefully to the one who has speech and language disorders.

• The children with speech and language disorders can enjoy the experience of listening to others, which means they can rest from the effort of talking, but still have an important and useful job to do, and can be assessed on a skill which forms part of the National Curriculum (English: speaking and listening skills).

Other children with different sorts of special needs can also start to participate in the normal lesson without having to rely on another adult — perhaps for the first time.

Many teachers have reported significant changes in self-esteem when children with special needs have started to participate as spotters, listeners, observers or feedback providers.

The initial verbal skills which are addressed in this chapter are intended to enable the children to become effective listeners who can recall accurately what they have heard, summarise the content and put it into their own words, that is, to paraphrase. This skill, initially taught verbally, is one which children are frequently called upon to use both verbally and in written form.

We constantly assess children's understanding by listening to their verbal recall and explanation of information that they have been given, either written or orally. Written examinations, at G.C.S.E., A level or even at degree level are based upon writing in your own words what you have been told and read to demonstrate that you know and understand the content.

Parroting

In order to teach the skill of paraphrasing it is useful to break this skill into sub-skills and teach the children the skills of parroting, summarising and clarifying which are useful in themselves, then put all the skills together into a paraphrase. Once they have done this the children will be in a position to choose appropriately from all four skills.

For this work we are going to use Attainment Target One (AT1) geographical skills, which focus on the skills of map-work, and encompasses the concepts of: place, position, proximity, distance, and sense of direction. These concepts are also needed for mathematics. MA 4 for example, talks of: position — level 1; movement — level 2; compass bearing — level 3; co-ordinates — level 4 and 5. This work in geography can therefore be specifically adapted for teacher assessment in maths.

It is useful to begin the work on place and direction with some personal talk about the children's homes. This acts as an orientation exercise and provides a good starting point for introducing the skill of

parroting.

It is very important that any work of a personal nature encompasses all possible permutations and that there is not a model of, say, two white Caucasian parents with two children living in a three-bedroomed house. Children soon pick up teacher models, and even quite confident children feel anxious if they suspect their situation does not fit the model. Over time this anxiety can lead to low self-esteem and poor academic work. It may manifest itself as a brash, arrogant 'don't care' approach, as well as a withdrawn, or less than enthusiastic response. Both behaviours can be interpreted as symptoms of a special need. Thus sensitivity towards plurality of family backgrounds and the encouragement of respect by children towards each other, which these structures try to establish, can act as preventative measures, in terms of difficult behaviour, in themselves. Additionally it is vital that children with a speech and language disorder feel comfortable with the content of the task; starting with a personal topic that is introduced with sensitivity should help to ensure that this is indeed the case. In time, as you begin to work in this way on a consistent basis, and as the children learn to trust one another, it may be possible for children to speak up for themselves and begin to articulate their anxieties about a topic.

Activity - Giving directions

Special needs context - speech and language disorders
Curriculum content - Geography AT1 - Map skills
Skills - attending behaviour

You make like to consider introducing the topic in this way:

Today we are going to do some work on places. We are going to start by talking about our homes: where they are, whether you have more than one home; how long you have lived where you live now; where and how to get there.

At the same time we are going to practise listening to each other and practise some skills which help us become really good listeners.

To help you get to know some more people in the class I want you to work with someone who is not necessarily your special friend. I have here some cards (use cards which have a picture of a house, road, park or something similar on them) which have been cut in half. Come and take a card and find someone who has the other half of your card then sit opposite them.

I want you first of all to take it in turns to tell the other person about your home. I want the person who is listening to show they are doing so with their bodies in the ways we have talked about and to try to help the other person to talk in whatever way you can. Be sure to use each others' names when you are encouraging the talker.

Tell younger children to describe their home(s). For older children

write some of the prompts on the board for them, for example; *how long have you lived in that home*, etc.

Allow about ten minutes for this activity, stop the children after five minutes and get them to exchange roles so that the listener talks about their house. Then ask them to stop, and check that they each had a turn and that the listener was using good eye contact.

It is useful to encourage them to give each other specific feedback in the sharing time even if they were not being observers or spotters, the best way to start this is by modelling.

Did anyone have a partner who they thought did really well at listening?
What did he do Donna ?
So Adam was a really good listener for you and he encouraged you by looking at you and leaning forward, is that right? Good.

The more you voice these kinds of statements the more the children will start to use them with each other. Such encouragement and feedback from both peers and teacher can be influential in altering the self-esteem of a child with special needs. For children with speech and language disorders positive and encouraging feedback on specific aspects of their speech from both peers and teachers can change both their confidence in their speech and their self-esteem.

Figure 5:1 Children sitting 'knee to knee' for a listening activity prior to parroting

Having reminded the children of the non-verbal behaviours, and orientated them into the topic, you can now focus the exercise on verbal skills.

Now I want you to each have a turn to say whether you find it easy to talk to other people or not and in what situations and to try to think of things that the people who you find it easy to talk to do. For example you may have noticed that it is easier to talk to your mother when you are reading a story together or when you are saying goodnight than when she is getting the tea. This will probably be because she looks at you and smiles. Think of the ways in which your partner helped you to talk about your homes just now. See how many different ways people can help you to talk, including the sorts of things they actually say.

Allow about fifteen minutes for this altogether, then ask the children to turn their chairs towards the front and share with the rest of the group the ideas they talked about.

Gather together the suggestions the children come up with by writing them on the board. The list may look like this:

> *smiling*
> *nodding*
> *saying: 'Yes, really, oh'*
> *saying: 'Did you like that? enjoy that?'*
> *not interrupting*
> *not saying: 'Oh yes, that happened to me too'*
> *saying: 'So you went to Sarah's house did you?'*

Activity - Lego directions

Special needs context - speech and language disorders
Curriculum content - Geography
Skills - Parroting

The last statement from the previous activity can be picked out as an example of parroting and commented on in the following kind of way:

So one way we can help someone to continue talking is to say back to them the exact words we have just heard, so that they know we have been listening, and they can continue just where they finished off without forgetting what they were going to say. This is called parroting because parrots tend to copy what they hear other people saying, they don't make up words for themselves.

Sometimes parroting can help the other person to say more clearly what they actually mean, because they hear their own words back and then say, 'Well no I didn't mean that you go down the road past the station exactly, I meant that as you go down the road you will see the road to the station.'

Sometimes people say things in a muffled way, sometimes you say things with your mouth full, some of you find it ever so hard to say something and still it doesn't seem to sound right. Someone being patient and listening, and the listener saying the words back to check to see if they got it right, will help in all these situations.

For your next piece of work I want one of you to try to tell the other one how to get to their house and for the listener to say the instructions back like a parrot. I want one of you to be left and one to be right, it doesn't matter who is which.

Lefts are to listen and practice parroting and rights are to come and collect a Lego person, a board, a piece of paper and some word cards.

If the children do not know their left and right stick a red sticker on the right hand and a lemon coloured sticker on the left hand, and explain the connection. Emphasise to the children the importance of using specialist words and tell them that knowledge of these words is essential for giving directions. Have some specialist word cards prepared in advance. Use words like crossroads, slope, river, hill, wood, park, as outlined in AT Level 2 but adapted to suit your neighbourhood. For older children it is helpful to use pictures to illustrate the words on the cards so that they have a visual prompt. For younger children who can't read you can use pictures only and reinforce orally. You may want the children to create pictures of these keywords themselves; this could be done in another context as an art activity, and the children's own drawings used on the cards. These could then be enlarged and displayed on the wall, with the written words displayed underneath. Tell the children that you are going to call them right and left.

'Rights', I want you to show your word cards to your partner and together make sure that you know what they mean. Then pick up your Lego person and the board and pretend the Lego person is your partner going from school to your house. Tell them how to get there and try to use some of the words on the card.

'Lefts', I want you to stop rights when you think you might forget the instruction and parrot back the instructions you heard them say.

Stop the children after about ten minutes and before they change roles ask lefts to go over the route again and to try to draw a map of the route.

Organise the children into a sharing circle again and ask them to share by having volunteers read out the instructions on how to get to their partner's home by following the map. It may be possible at this point to draw out from the language disordered child and their partner the usefulness of parroting for them, by asking for comments from the whole class on that activity before they are directed towards the next activity.

When several children have done this draw out some of the phrases connected with location and proximity and write them on the board, e.g.

It's the road by the church.
It's near the bridge.
Turn left at the chip shop.
The road is called Burder Street.

This is in preparation for some map work during their next lesson.

Make sure that the children have the map of the route to their own homes and not that of their partners to put away in their drawers. Tell them to notice some of these landmarks on their way home from school tonight.

Summarising

Summarising is the art of pulling together the main points that have been made by the speaker; a good summary takes account of some of the detail initially offered. A two-line summary of a five minute statement can be experienced as a put down by the speaker, and the intention of the listener is always to help the speaker not to leave them feeling let down, so it is important that children learn to summarise with sensitivity. Again this is a skill that would often help things along if used in staff meetings, governors' meetings, assessment agreement trials and so on. However the reason we as adults are often unable to use such skills to good effect is not because the skill is particularly difficult but because we have not had much practice. Introducing this skill to even quite young children means that they are more likely to be able to use it well in group work and discussions. It is a skill which is often associated with a leadership function; often in meetings the summarising is left to the chairperson. Children with special educational needs using this skill are likely to be regarded as leaders and people with something to offer rather than passive members. Children with speech and language disorders may well find new confidence in their role as listener, as they may find it easier to summarise than to express their own thoughts, although the environment will be safe and encouraging when it is their turn to be the speaker.

It is probably the adults in the children's lives who usually summarise for them, so you could introduce the idea of summarising by giving them an example of times that they have given you a detailed description or request and you have offered them a summary. In particular you can offer the children the phrase:
'... so *what you are saying is* ...'
You can also define a summary as making something short that was long, but making sure that you include all the ideas that the speaker covered. The link with the previous skill is that you need to remember some of the words the speaker used, as with parroting, but not every single one, unlike parroting.

Children are often asked to summarise for the first time in a piece of writing which is quite a sophisticated skill. Introducing summary skills orally in this way means that even young children can become quite proficient at summarising before they begin to write.

Activity - Using map symbols

Special needs context - speech and language disorders
Curriculum content - Geography AT1 - Map symbols
Skill - summarising

Organise the children into random pairs again and ask them to get out the maps they did in the previous activity. Ask them to take it in turns to tell each other the way home again, using the map but with them adding in the landmarks they noticed on their way home. This would act as an orientation and revision lesson and as an introduction for the skill of summarising.

When the speaker has finished talking about their route, with the additional landmarks, the job of the listener is to summarise by repeating back the main features of the route.

Another activity which can be used to reinforce the idea of summarising is to link the concept of map symbols with verbal summary. The symbol on a map is a shortened form of a landmark, indeed a map is a shortened representation of a set of descriptions. Thus map-work symbols and summary skills fit neatly together. Introduce the idea of map symbols by having some copies of an Ordnance Survey map of the neighbourhood enlarged, include the key to the symbols and ask the children if they can find some of the symbols on the map, for example a church, their school, a hospital. A general discussion on symbols around us, for example MacDonalds, Esso, Midland Bank etc, may help.

In the next geography session organise the children into random fours. Give them a large sheet of paper and some crayons and ask them to draw as many different symbols for the landmarks they recorded on their maps, or talked about in their directions to their home, as they can. Emphasise that these may be ones they have seen on maps or they may be their own made up ones. You could then share the various ideas they come up with, and ask them to draw the symbol and word on two pieces of small card to use for random pairs at a later stage.

Ask the children to work in pairs and to go through a new route e.g. round the school, playground or classroom, one talking and one summarising by writing down the route in symbol form as below. They can then work with another pair, to try and decode each other's symbolled routes. The links with verbal summary skills need to be emphasised all the way through.

This work on maps and routes prepares the children for AT Level 2/c: follow a route or trail round the school site or a nearby open space and Level 3/c: make a map of the route to school or a trail round the school site.

Clarifying

This skill is particularly useful for the language disordered child because they can learn to say something in new words, with the help of their partner's comments.

Activity - The Mad Professor and the Robot

Special needs context - speech and language disorders

Curriculum content - Geography AT1 and Ma 4 - Directions

Skill - clarifying

For this exercise organise the students into random groups of three. Explain to them that you are going to practise two things today, one is the skill of clarifying and the other is the skill of giving clear directions. You may say something along these lines

The listening skill we are going to practise today is called clarifying. It is a mixture of parroting and summarising because you use new words as you do with summary but you are checking out as we did with parroting.

The geography skill we are going to practise is that of giving directions in a small space, like a classroom.

First I want you to practice clarifying, in your threes. Sit so that one of you is slightly apart and can observe the other two who will take it in turns to be speaker and clarifier. Speaker, I want you to think of your favourite toy or possession at home, to remember where it is and then to tell the clarifier where it is. Clarifier, you are to keep asking questions to get the speaker to be more exact. 'So it is in the toy cupboard?' 'Yes.' 'On which shelf?' 'On the third.' 'What is it next to?' Observer, you are to make sure that the clarifier is doing what I have said and to tell them how well they did it.

Allow the children about 15 minutes for this, depending on their age, i.e. with older children it may take 30 minutes and you can do the robot exercise below another day. Ask them how easy or difficult it was to clarify. Ask the observers for some examples of good clarifying; What exactly did they do or say? Record some examples of good clarifying phrases on the board, then organise the children in their threes into the robot exercise.

Now I want one of you to be a robot a bit like the Romar toy, one of you to be a mad professor, and one an observer.

It doesn't matter who is which because you will all change over and get a chance to be each of the roles. Now mad professor it is your job to give instructions to the robot. For example: 'Go straight ahead for ten paces, stop, turn right, stop ...' Robot, you check out the instructions and try to clarify them, 'You want me to go straight for ten paces then stop then turn right, then what do I do?' You are a special robot who can ask questions, not just one that repeats instructions. The observer is to remind the robot to clarify, and to remind the professor to use some of the special words we have been learning, for example junction, crossroad, north and south.

Older children can use a tally sheet to record likely questions, this can then link in with the maths curriculum as mentioned earlier, where criteria for data collection for direction, distance and proximity can be met. This exercise should serve as an introduction to clarifying and a revision for the work on direction.

Activity - Weather

Special needs context - speech and language disorders
Curriculum content - Geography AT3 Weather
Skill - clarifying

A way of consolidating the clarifying skill would be to practise it again with a new geography topic, following a week of weather watching. Children will have recorded weather observations: wet and dry, hot and cold; wind direction etc. Younger children can use simple observations: *Is it hot today? Yes,* tick the sun column. Older children can use temperature and rain gauge instruments, reading degrees and millilitres.

Organise the children into random pairs, using the weather symbols (figure 5.2). Ask the pair to describe the weather for one of the days, then to tell another pair. The listening pair then use their clarifying skills to try to draw a weather map like the weather person has on television. (You could use a video clipping of the weather forecast in case some of the children haven't seen it before.)

This exercise could also be used to reinforce summary skills. Be sure to make it clear to the children which skill it is you want them to practise though and ensure that they know the difference in behavioural terms. Use spotters to look out for good examples of listening behaviour and to give specific feedback.

Paraphrasing

The skill of paraphrasing as indicated earlier is a synthesis of the elements of parroting, summarising and clarifying. A good paraphrase will act as a summary by interrupting the flow of the speaker to check that the listener has understood so far, it will use the speaker's words but in a shortened form; it may well seek clarification on some points. A good paraphrase helps the speaker to order their thoughts and sometimes to gain insight into their own actions or motivations. It is a fundamental skill in counselling, so by teaching it we are equipping children with the skills they need to counsel each other. Paraphrasing is a key skill for appraisal, where it helps the appraisee reflect on their work and their achievements. It is also valuable in discipline situation where children can be encouraged to reflect on their behaviour rather than be immediately chastised. It is useful for the record of achievement and assessment interview and it is useful for the speech and language disordered child as both a speaker and a listener.

For initial practice in paraphrasing it is useful to follow the format

Figure 5:2 Weather symbols for random pairs

outlined in the sections above, that is to allow the children to talk about something personal in their lives, in pairs, with the listener practising the skill of paraphrasing which has been carefully described by you. It is important that children are reminded of the importance of picking out the main points but also including some detail so that the speaker does not feel dismissed in one sentence. It may be that many opportunities for practice are provided so that the children can learn to distinguish between main points and detail.

Once the children have had some practice they can then combine the skill with the geography content. An exercise that does this is outlined below.

Activity - Using maps

Special needs context - speech and language disorders
Curriculum content - Geography AT1 Using maps
Skill - paraphrasing

Organise the children into random pairs. Use the landmark and its symbol that the children made in their summary exercise, these cards can then be used for assessment purposes later on. Tell the children that you want them to imagine their ideal home; they have a magic wand and they can make it anywhere and however they like. Tell them to concentrate on the position; *where* is it exactly; near a stream, up a mountain, on a hill, on an island? What would you see if you were looking out of the windows? Tell the children that while some of the exercise is creative, you will be going around listening out for words of description of place, for their geography and for words of a good paraphrase for their communication skills. In this way you have shared the criteria for success with the children, they know what it is you are looking for and they can show off their skills to the best of their ability. The paraphrasing gives the speech and language disordered child an opportunity to reflect on their choice of word and to restate using words of place if they choose.

After each child has taken a turn, organise them into fours, each pair working with another pair, and ask the partner to describe the ideal home of the one they listened to. After each description the two new partners paraphrase the description they have just heard. This work could be followed up with some written accounts and drawings of the ideal homes, highlighting key words of place for future recall.

This set of exercises could be rounded off by taking the group out, either around the school or in the neighbourhood. Working in pairs they could follow instructions on a sheet with a map, or a trail devised by classmates, using the landmark words practised throughout. For children who cannot read the instructions could be on tape recorder.

For younger children the blind trust walk could be used; one of the pair closes their eyes or else has a blindfold on depending on their personal preference (some young children find blindfolds frightening), the other acts as the eyes, by holding their arm and giving instructions of directions, and descriptions of the surroundings, particularly obstacles. Once children have practised this in the classroom they may like to practise down the corridors, out in the playground or even further afield.

Older children could be set the task of devising a treasure trail, or a nature hunt for the younger ones, again with criteria of descriptions of place.

Children followed up the activity by creating a map quiz for other groups in the class. They used these sheets to record the questions, answers and co-ordinates. This was used as the answer sheet. They then produced a copy of the sheet where they had missed out either co-ordinates or the name of the feature or both, to form a quiz sheet (fig 5.3). The groups then swapped their quiz sheets, looked for the answers and co-ordinates on the maps and swapped them back to be marked by the first group. An alternative follow up activity was given when pairs created their own maps on a map grid (fig 5.4) and then recorded their position on the sheet (fig 5.5). The sheets were then used to effect an instructions activity, where one pair tried to describe their map to another using co-ordinates to create identical maps.

Find six different features on your map. Number 1 is given as an example. Think of a good question to ask about the features and landmarks. Write down the name of your landmark, your question and the co-ordinates. This sheet is your answer sheet.

When you have made up your quiz copy your questions onto new sheet and give this to another group.

Feature / Landmark and question.	East/West co-ordinates	North/South co-ordinates
1. Find the town with a railway station. What is the name of the town ?		
2.		
3.		
4.		
5.		
6.		

THE MAP USED FOR THIS QUIZ WAS;   SCALE;

Figure 5:3 A map quiz sheet

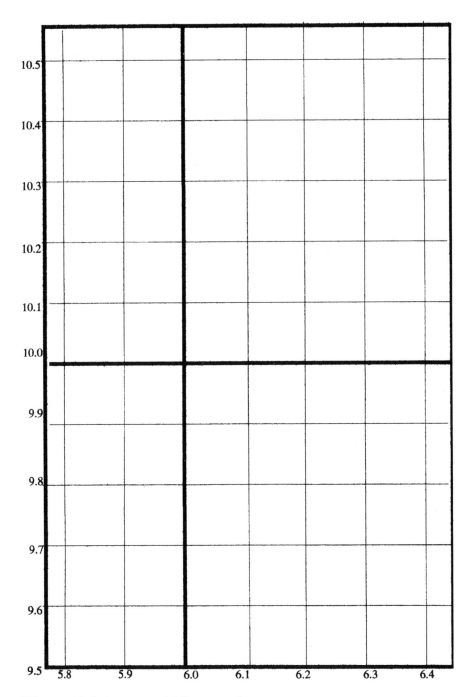

Figure 5:4 A map grid for creating your own map

1. Look at the nine features on the map you have created. Record their positions on the grid below.

2. Use the grid to give instructions to draw a map to another pair. Check whether the map they have drawn is the same as yours.

Ordinance Survey Symbol	Landmark	N / S co-ordinates	E / W co-ordinates
1.			
2.			
3.			
4.			
5.			
6.			
7.			
8.			
9.			

Figure 5:5 A co-ordinates sheet for using with the map grid

CHAPTER 6

Types of Talk

Children need to understand the different types of talk that they can use and be given the opportunity to explore and practise different types in different situations.

Activity - Collecting data

Special needs context - learning difficulties
Curriculum content - Maths data collection
Skill - using a variety of talk

A very simple exercise to help them understand the different types of talk used in the classroom, which is also is part of data collection in the maths National Curriculum is to complete an observational survey within their own classroom or in another classroom in the school. It is best that the children work in small groups. For this first activity they can observe without taking any written note of the talk, although some may choose to do so. Their task is to listen and come up with a list of types of talk that they observed. As a group they need to then share their lists and put them together to create categories of talk which can be used in an observation schedule. The advantage of the children creating the schedule in this way is that they are assured that all the children understand which type of talk fits into which category because they have created the divisions themselves. It also models the system which is commonly used to create and carry out surveys, which they might later wish to do on an individual basis (Ma 5/5b).

You may, however, wish to use a prepared observation sheet like figure 6.1 with the children to illustrate the type of observation sheet they might design.

The group can then design an observation schedule to use on a second occasion. This will provide an opportunity to teach the children about different types of schedules and the uses and advantages of each, e.g. timed intervals or frequency. The group might decide to all carry out the same schedule for the same period, or each carry out the same schedule for consecutive periods, or they

TYPES OF TALK	PUPILS	TEACHER
ASKING QUESTIONS		
ANSWERING		
ASKING FOR EQUIPMENT		
CHATTING		
DISCUSSING WORK		

Figure 6:1 Types of talk observation sheet

might wish to create schedules which would involve each child looking for a different type of talk. This decision allows a discussion on the 'fairness' and reliability of the observation, both of which are important for maths and science.

Following the children's own observations of the type of talk in school they might be asked to observe talk in different situations outside the school. This could give an opportunity for children to demonstrate their learning and understanding of the schedules used in class and create an ideal assessment opportunity for the teacher, as each child's schedule would show the level of understanding through the level of sophistication shown.

This activity will raise the children's awareness of the different types of talk. They will have already begun to recognise through observation of the talk of others the types of talk they themselves use in different situations. Many children will find that they are very good at talking in one particular situation but are not so good in another. Some children will realise that they very rarely talk in school at all. Others may find that they do not know how to shut up! The teacher and pupils may both become more aware of what it is about some children that makes them demanding, frustrating or annoying. Some children (and adults) are good talkers but they often talk inappropriately, i.e. are talking when they should listen, are asking questions when they should be giving information, are silent when they should be contributing. It is possible that both pupils and teachers react to each other's talk patterns without knowing that is what they are doing. The result might be a dislike for each other which appears without foundation.

The children now need time and opportunities to practise different skills in order to be able to use a variety of types of talk, at the most appropriate times.

Talking about ourselves

Many students who are reluctant to talk in school are responding to past experiences which have taught them that in school there is a right or a wrong answer. Even when a teacher asks what seems to be an open question there is an awareness that there is an answer which the teacher holds in their head and it is the students' task to guess what that answer is. Listening to teachers conducting question and answer sessions it becomes clear that some plausible answers are dismissed because they do not fit the model answer in the teacher's mind. Saying 'what you think' becomes 'out-guess the teacher'. This was very aptly illustrated by the 1991 and 1992 SATs where at both Key Stage 1 and Key Stage 3 there were model answers which the children needed to give in order to demonstrate 'success'. In practice, children gave other answers which were equally sophisticated and even showed greater understanding but did not fit in with the model answer given. These imposed 'tests' seem to mirror a quite common teaching style.

If we want students to change from being reluctant talkers to ones who can contribute and discuss more freely, the notion that what they say can be judged right or wrong needs to be removed. The best possible way to do this is to allow children to talk about themselves. They are the world's authority on themselves; no one can be wrong about what they themselves think and feel; they know all about their own habits, hobbies, successes and failures. Structured talk about themselves can be followed up or preceded by work on a Hobbies folder, initially using prompt sheets to collect or record their thoughts. One author used such sheets to allow children to conduct formal interviews about children's hobbies, which were recorded by the interviewer and then given back to the interviewee, to enable them to write a detailed account of their hobbies and interest for a Record of Achievement folder.

Figure 6:2 Front sheet for a Hobbies Folder

```
Interview questions for 'My Hobby' Topic

What is your hobby or interest?

What do you do to take part in your hobby?

Do you do this on your own or with other people? If
with other people who are they?

When do you do your hobby?

How often?

Where do you do your hobby?

What equipment do you need?

How much does it cost?

Is your hobby organised by adults or do you organise
it yourself?

Who helps you with your hobby?

What is the best thing about your hobby?

Have you any other different hobbies or interests?

What else do you think you could put in your hobby
topic that would make it interesting? e.g. photocopies
of medals and certificates; photographs of yourself;
pieces of magazines or catalogues; newspaper
cuttings;..........................................................................

What would be the best design for the cover of your
folder?
```

Figure 6.3 Prompt questions for an interview

Talkers need listeners

The other feature which helps students to talk is to have someone who is listening. There is nothing more frustrating than talking when no one is listening to you. Students who have been taught active listening skills, as above, will be enabling other students to talk more effectively. Summarising and paraphrasing the other speaker helps that person to clarify what it is they are saying and moves them on to further talk. Asking questions which encourage further exploration of a subject is another important technique for children to learn and use.

Asking questions and giving answers

Asking questions and giving answers are two important aspects of a learning process. In school it has traditionally been the teacher doing the telling (giving out information) and the students doing the asking (asking questions when they don't understand) or the teacher doing the asking (questioning students on what they have been told or are studying) and the students telling (giving them the answers). This allows the teacher to control the information being given out to ensure that it is correct. It also allows the teacher to control the talk very effectively but it means that only one person can talk at any one time. For the teacher this is a very tiring process as they are in demand all the time and the need for teachers to 'know everything' is clear.

For the student with special needs this might cause problems and anxieties. The student might well need extra time and attention. This causes both embarrassment to the student and a feeling of frustration and unfairness to the teacher. Teachers wish to give all students equal time, even if they cannot do so in practice. This has been dealt with in the past by the use of support teachers. The labelling effect of this type of support might outweigh the advantages of the extra time and attention given to the student. For some students the effect of a separate teacher for them means that when they are successful as learners they are unable to attribute that success to themselves, and they will come to believe that the only way they can achieve success is through the work, effort and ability of the teacher rather than themselves.

The alternative is for students to talk to each other, with the peer group providing an opportunity to ask questions, give answers and check out information. This means that all the students can participate in the activity, including those with special needs, and the teacher is freed to support any student, or group of students who need further information or help.

There are clear advantages for all members of a class group. Those students who have previous knowledge of a subject can use that knowledge to help others. This will be of benefit to their own understanding, as they clarify their own thoughts when teaching someone else. It also benefits those to whom the information is given, as it provides one-to-one tuition on this new information. This one-to-one model then becomes the same for all the students, not just those with special needs. This is very important for their feelings of inclusion within the classroom.

If students are to be enabled to talk to each other in this way and be effective learners through that process they need to be taught the skills of 'asking'. They need to be able to ask questions which elicit factual information; which allow the other person to express personal opinions and feelings; which are open in nature and allow the other person to explore an issue more fully. They also need to be able to ask for help.

The same students need to be taught how to 'tell' others. This might be the giving of factual information in a form which is concise and easy to understand or giving more detailed explanation of events or theories. They might need to explore aloud their thoughts and express their feelings and opinions on a subject, either personal or academic; they might need to support another person's learning by helping another to arrive at the correct solution without giving them the answer, or correcting whilst praising.

Asking open and closed questions

Activity - Conducting an interview

Special needs context - learning difficulties

Curriculum content - Science AT2 and English AT1 and 3

Skill - asking closed and open questions

Explain to the children that they are going to be learning two things at once. They are going to practise asking different types of questions, which they might use later to interview people. They are also going to be using descriptive language orally in order to help them become better at writing descriptions (En 3 - Writing).

Divide the children into random groups so there are about five or six groups in the class. Each group is to talk together and decide on an animal that they are going to be. Each group then thinks of two questions that they will ask another group, which can only be answered with *yes* or *no* (e.g. Do you eat grass?). These are closed questions. Sit the children in a circle with each group sitting together within the circle. With each person in an animal group answering just one question each in turn the rest of the class ask their questions. This version of 'Twenty Questions' illustrates very clearly the type of wording which might encourage a one word answer. After all the questions are answered the class may try to guess the animal. This activity can be varied with different topics to guess, different size groups and different scoring systems.

Following the traditional yes/no answers, ask the groups to choose an object that they are going to be. This time they have to think of two questions which will encourage the speaker to give them longer

Figure 6:4 Groups asking each other questions

answers. The circle time of asking the groups then proceeds as before with the object being guessed at the end of the round (or before, if appropriate).

Ask the children in their small groups to talk about the differences in the questions, the answers and how easy it was to talk in the two different questioning situations. It is important that they have an opportunity to talk about the implications of the exercise in relation to work in school and life in general. Points to draw out from the whole class at the end of this discussion might be the use of these questions in interviewing for surveys, asking questions in the class, clarifying what they need to know with adults and peers, and encouraging others to talk more freely to them.

The asking and answering skills will be recognised by teachers as the tools of the trade. They are however important skills for all adults, whatever their job. They can and should be taught to students and they can be taught in such a way that they help the teacher to manage the classroom effectively. They are very important to those students with special needs and for those students who will be working alongside them.

Once the children are asking questions more readily of a wide variety of classroom participants, they can monitor their own performance using spotters sheets (see fig 4.2) or specific schedules which record the frequency of asking questions.

Asking questions

Names of the children	1.		2.	3.		4.
ASKING QUESTIONS	ASKING THE TEACHER	ASKING THE OTHER TEACHER	ASKING A FRIEND	ASKING ANOTHER PUPIL	OTHERS	
9.30 - 9.40						
10 -10.10						
10.30-10.40						
11 - 11.10						
11.30 - 11.40						

Figure 6:5 Schedule for recording observations on asking questions

Using questioning in the curriculum

It is important that, having been alerted to the variety of talk and questioning available to them, the children are given an opportunity within the curriculum to use and practise the skills taught in the above activities.

Activity - Water

Special needs context - learning difficulties
Curriculum content - Science AT2 and 3
Skills - Asking for and giving information

Explain to the children that over the next two sessions (possibly a day or day and a half) they will be learning two different things; first all about water, and secondly, how to ask good questions to find out what they want to know and how to give answers that are easy for everyone to understand.

Ask the children to sit in a circle and begin with a 'Water is ...' stem statement. Each child in turn says 'Water is ...' completing the statement in any way they want. Statements can be repeated or smaller circles of about eight might be used. It is important for the collective view of water to be established. Children then get into pairs. They are going to conduct an interview with another pair. Ask them to think of some questions about the water in their bodies (blood, sweat, tears, urine, amniotic fluid etc.), the ways in which they use water, the times they remember being in or near water. The teacher might wish to give a finite number of questions or leave that open to the children. As a pair they are to take turns in asking each other these questions. After each question is asked they are to talk about how easy it was to answer and how it might be altered to make it better at getting the information. Adjustments to the question can then be noted.

After their questions have been refined, the pair can join another pair and they make two new pairs. Each person is then to interview the other using the questions they have composed.

Finally the two pairs reform into a four, armed with both the answers to the questions they asked and the answers they gave to the questions they were asked by the others. The four can then be asked to make a presentation 'Water is ...' to the rest of group in any way they choose (drawings, drama, verbal, writing or a mixture). Make it clear that the whole group must be involved in their presentation. Give a short time for preparation and just a few minutes time limit for the presentation itself. The variety of presentation styles allows children with severe learning difficulties to be involved fully but not regarded as a hindrance if they are unable to write or talk. The children themselves need to be encouraged to find the type of presentation which will use everybody's abilities and talents to the best advantage. Praise the way in which the children work together, the use of different, clear or unusual presentation methods, their use of all the group, as well as the information they have gleaned about water. Ask the rest of the 'audience' to comment and give feedback on the clarity of the presentation.

If you have to 'do class assemblies' these presentations offer a ready made assembly for the children to 'perform' with absolutely no aggravation to the teacher. Alternatives might include each group of four being given a card with a different slant on water, e.g. Water and the world, Water and me, Water and animals, Water and our school, etc.

For the following session the teacher could set up, for a class of 30 to 32 children, four different water experiments for the children to work on. Each four formed the previous day can join with another four. Explain to the children that there will be two tasks going on simultaneously. First they will be carrying out an experiment and they will be asked later to say what they found out. Second they will be being observed by the other group to see how well they ask and answer questions. The first four will then carry out the experiment, from instructions either written on a card or taped. The partners will use an observation checklist or make notes or just observe (See figs 4.2, 6.1)

The fours then swap roles and repeat the experiment. There should be a strict time boundary for the experiment so that the whole class is managed together. Groups that don't finish will have the opportunity to glean that knowledge from groups that do. Make sure that the time given is sufficient but not too long and be prepared to be flexible if need be. Give some time at the end of each session for the whole eight to talk about what they found out about water and what they observed about each others' questions and answers. Ensure that they give feedback on the way in which everybody was or wasn't included in the group.

Older children could conduct experiments such as dissolving different solids in water, testing and describing different liquids for their PH number and viscosity, looking at and recording refraction (mirrors and rainbows, bending pencils), taking the temperature of ice, ice and salt, room temperature water and boiling water/steam. A teacher could 'hover' to ensure the safety of the children whilst assessing the visiting groups.

With young children the absorbency of different materials could be a possible experiment, using water as the liquid; or they could blow water round a calibrated tube to measure the capacity of the lungs, or use timers and water dripping to calibrate a series of containers, or add water to spread different types of ink on blotting paper. There are many other possibilities. This would cover much of Sc 1, Sc 3, and Ma 5. As the groups would be maintained and observed throughout by their peers, the teacher might choose to assess either a particular attainment target or a particular group of children.

CHAPTER 7

Children with Emotional and Behavioural Difficulties

Attention-seeking behaviour

Children with emotional and behavioural difficulties have special needs. Whatever the initial cause of difficulty in school — academic failure or feelings of social difference — these children have come to feel different and less valued. As a result of feeling different children begin to behave in negative, destructive ways. This acting out is what teachers recognise as attention-seeking behaviour. The children are indeed seeking attention by using 'bad behaviour' as they feel they are unable to behave well and so are receiving little reward for good behaviour. This attention seeking is very difficult to deal with in the classroom. Teachers are faced with a choice; ignoring the behaviour, which does nothing to encourage the children to change; or responding to the attention seeking with anger or disapproval, which reinforces the behaviour because it has achieved it purpose and gained the teacher's attention.

Labelling difficult children

When children behave badly in school it is very easy for teachers to begin to feel negatively about them. Teachers may notice the difference in behaviour of all the class when that child is away. This leads to the assumption that the problem is the child. This might well lead to the teacher labelling that child as difficult, disruptive, 'hyperkinetic', naughty, or low ability.

The problem with labelling the child is that it does not tell you anything about what that child actually does. A behaviour, such as answering back, might be seen as disruptive and rude by one teacher, whilst another sees it as showing creativity. Research shows that the effects of labelling children are that the child performs according to the label. A child who a teacher perceives as being a thief or clumsy will be the one most likely to be accused when something is stolen or broken. From the child's perspective, since they feel that they cannot win because they are often accused of things they haven't done, it seems that they have little to lose by behaving as badly as the teacher thinks that they do.

In fact they may behave more badly than that or be set up and blamed by the other children who begin to share the teacher's expectations. In the authors' experience, this can happen on a whole school basis. For example a child who tends to be clumsy may become well known to all the other members of staff. If there is a slight disruption in a whole school assembly, close to that child, he or she might well be told off by a teacher who might not know the child, but only his or her reputation. This frequently happens with lunchtime supervisors, who rely heavily on reputations and know few of the children really well. Much needs to be done to eradicate this whole school labelling.

The motivation for bad behaviour

There are other ways of looking at troublesome behaviour which allow more constructive outcomes. The psychology we find most useful and helpful in working with these children is that all behaviour is purposeful for the one who owns the behaviour. For example, a child who hits another child or destroys their work may be seen by the teacher as a bully or a mindless vandal. There seems to be no reason behind these acts. When a counsellor or behaviour specialist works with such children, our experience is that the children can explain the reasons for their act quite lucidly. In most cases the reasons given are within our own experience and are easy to understand. A child who hits another might be responding to a previous comment by the 'victim' about his work, family or personal hygiene. Destruction of another child's work might seem mindless but upon investigation the child will usually reveal that this is an act of vengeance, based upon incidents which the teacher may well have forgotten, but the child hasn't.

The implication of this for teachers is that to pre-judge another's motive may lead to very little understanding of the reasons behind the behaviour. The judgement is that the child is one that 'just behaves badly'. Teachers need to ensure that they listen to the child to ensure that they have a better perspective on the child's motivation. This is what the behaviour specialist will do. They will listen carefully to what the child says in order to better understand what it is that is motivating the child to behave in a particular way. What behaviour specialists recognise is that all of us seek and need approval. If we feel we cannot get approval in an institution then attention through disapproval is better than no attention at all.

Therefore when children are 'acting out' it is useful to bear in mind that whilst it might feel like a personal attack, it is not personal to that teacher. It may well be the role of teacher that they are rebelling against. Viewing personal attacks and discipline problems in this way can help teachers to see that winning a battle with the child is less important than relating positively with them and gaining insight into their motives.

Many teachers feel that they do not have the specialist skills of behaviour specialist or counsellor, nor do they have the time to work in a one to one way with difficult children. In fact they might well be feeling resentful about the time already spent dealing with that child. The best solution may appear to be the removal of the child. Looked at from the child's perspective, they are already acting this way because they feel different, so removal is the worst thing that could possibly happen, because they will feel even more different.

Identifying and expressing feelings

Children who experience failure and rejection, and who have already resorted to behaving badly as their only option, are very vulnerable to further failure. They have learnt to cut off from their real feelings because they hurt so much. They protect themselves by putting up a facade of not caring and use the language of bravado, when faced with punishment like exclusion. The punishments therefore do not work. The irony is that you do not need to punish them, because they are punishing themselves more cruelly than any teacher or institution. They need to experience both success and acceptance. They need to be taught the steps involved in behaving well, because they are in the habit of behaving badly. They need to learn how to experience their real feelings again. They can do this by talking about them. For this they need a trusting environment where they feel accepted by their teacher and peers. This allows them to feel safe enough to explore and talk about their real selves.

An excellent way of getting children with emotional and behavioural difficulties to explore their feelings and to become involved with the curriculum and with other children in the class, is through drama. Drama is also a useful medium in the history curriculum for encouraging empathy and feeling for life in past times.

Children do need to explore their feelings and so do teachers. This may feel very risky to teachers who are in the habit, out of self preservation, of acting a part in front of the class. In order to maintain discipline many teachers act as if they are angry, happy or kind. Children are very good at spotting the difference between real and pretend anger! The problem for teachers is the feeling of loss of personal control when their feelings are experienced and displayed. There are feelings of being vulnerable. In fact, teachers are very similar to the children they teach in this respect.

Being genuine

It is important, however, that the teacher is genuine about the feelings that they display in the classroom. They need to look for something in the children that they can genuinely like, encourage and respect, as these children are often very sensitive to genuineness or lack of it.

Being genuine allows the development of the positive classroom ethos. This is vital if children with emotional and behavioural difficulties are going to risk sharing their own feelings in a safe and trusting environment. We have found that teachers who share their own feelings are able to get through to difficult, closed down children. If a teacher says to a child, 'I'm sorry', 'I feel sad that you did that!', 'I feel angry when you do that!', the child hears a genuine response from the teacher. They are also provided with an appropriate model of how they can deal with difficult and frustrating situations that make them feel sad, angry or sorry.

It is the skill of describing the behaviour of the child, not labelling the child, and the skill of stating your own feelings that result from that behaviour, that form the basis of the 'I' statements. In our experience, the use of these statements is very effective with children with emotional and behavioural difficulties. The use of the broken record technique and 'I' statements to deal with conflict, are outlined in detail in chapter two.

Giving children responsibility

With this framework for understanding behaviour it becomes clear that the best way to help children with emotional and behavioural difficulties is to give them ways of gaining approval without acting out. One of the best ways we know of doing that is to make this child a monitor or helper, to enlist their help. This can be both 'helping' you, the teacher, and 'helping' the group to achieve its goal.

At this point many teachers may say, 'That's easier said than done. How can we trust such children when their behaviour is so poor?' Clearly such children need strictly defined targets and clear boundaries drawn. We recommend procedures such as negotiated class rules — with the whole class drawing up and agreeing to a set of rules, which are then clearly displayed.

One of the best ways to start the work of responsibility with these children is to give them a partner to tutor — either a peer of the same age or a younger age student. At first it will be sufficient to allow the two to work together but as time goes on the tutor child will need 'giving help' skills and 'teaching others' skills. The questioning and interviewing techniques outlined below are sub-sets of these skills.

History and interactive learning

Talking to teachers we have found that many of them feel that teaching history is not straightforward. The skills required to be a good historian are quite complex. They include an awareness of time lines, which many people feel is quite difficult for young children to grasp, a retention of specific factual details, an ability to analyse cause and effect and an ability to imagine what it might have been like to live in those days; in other words, empathy. There is also a feeling that since the majority of information is outside the children's experience it means they have to read or listen first before they can progress with an activity.

Traditionally teachers have often approached history teaching through using video, television or stories as a stimulus for a project or followed up with worksheets. The project often involves the children in finding and copying information from books. Even with differentiated worksheets, many are based upon comprehension or recall techniques. Such approaches may be excellent for teaching factual detail, but they do not address issues of time, analysis of cause and effect, or empathy, which are important elements of the history National Curriculum. Children who have difficulties with reading and writing find the traditional approach to history daunting and unhelpful. Whether projects or worksheets are used, there is an element of competition. This may be doing the best or neatest project or getting it all correct. Either way, the children have to try to keep up with each other and this leads inevitably to failure for many, success for some and frustration at being held back for others. A lose — lose situation! It is our experience that children make the best progress when they are allowed to go at their own pace without feeling that they are behind in their work compared to others or that they are holding others up.

The children who fail in history because of the way it is traditionally presented will come to dislike the subject and feel that they are failing yet again. The feelings of failure are often transferred to other subject areas, as the children assimilate them into their self image. Research demonstrates that it is these very children who are failing academically who display emotional and behavioural difficulties in school (Lund, 1987).

Children with emotional and behavioural difficulties benefit from being given responsibility such as teaching someone else in a peer tutoring situation and organising or having a role in a group. Children clearly need to acquire historical information. There are alternatives to the traditional approach of the teacher as the sole provider of historical fact and information. It seems to us therefore that one excellent way of approaching history is to help the children to work in small research groups and then to exchange information. This way of learning can be extremely successful and interesting for all the children, including those with reading difficulties and recording problems. In order for children to be able to work in this way, they need to have certain skills relating to research methods and group skills.

Research and interviewing

The skills outlined in the previous chapters are an excellent foundation for teaching skills for group work. The skills children need for research in groups are primarily listening and questioning. These interviewing skills, once acquired, have many other applications for studying historical topics, for example: interviewing members of the community, local historians, museum workers, local archaeologists. They are skills which can be transferred to other curriculum areas, such as science and technology.

For us, research is not based purely on finding information from written sources alone, but is a broader concept, involving children with primary and secondary source material. These might be artifacts such as pottery, bone, and manuscripts or photographs of such items.

The role of the teacher in this approach is not to gather the information for the children and present it in an easy-to-digest fashion, but to gather together many and various source materials. It does not matter whether these materials were originally designed for adults or children, are easy or hard, simple or complex. The museum education service and the library service can often be helpful agencies for acquiring artifacts and other source materials on a loan basis. If teachers wish these agencies to put together project boxes then notification should be given well in advance.

The variety of source materials is important if the teacher is to enthuse children who have learning or emotional and behavioural difficulties. This might include visits out of school to museums or sites. These need to be considered carefully. Trips that are over long allow children to become bored and then behave badly. Worksheets given to children on trips can be inhibiting to children who have difficulties with learning through the written medium. In fact, teachers may find that even those children who have no difficulty in reading will become turned off by worksheets or so involved in getting the right answer to the few questions posed, that they miss a great deal of the other opportunities to look, examine and learn.

Activity - Egypt

Special needs context - emotional and behavioural difficulty
Curriculum content - history; Egypt
Skills - questioning and Interviewing

For this first session on Eygpt you will need to have some sugar paper and crayons, enough for one sheet for each group of four and several crayons for each sheet.

Tell the children that the topic they are going to explore next is Eygpt. Mention the fact that the word pyramid is often the one that comes to mind in connection with Eygpt. You may want to get one child to briefly draw a pyramid shape on the board, particularly with younger children, so that we all know what we are talking about — this is an ideal opportunity to give the child with emotional and behavioural difficulties some responsibility. Then tell the children that you want them to arrange themselves in a line by height, like the side of a pyramid. When they have done this you can ask them to make a pair with the person standing next to them so that they are in random pairs.

Tell the children to sit in their pairs in their listening or knee to knee positions. Ask them to take it in turns to say how hard or difficult they found it to make the pyramid line. It is hard to do whole group co-operative activities, and they should be told this, and congratulated on their ability to do it. This type of personal reviewing — How well did my group do at that task and how well did I do? — is known as processing and is a useful habit to get children into. It allows feelings of frustration to be expressed, and encourages behavioural goal setting. Both these skills are useful ones for all children to learn but are particularly useful for children with emotional and behavioural difficulties.

You may like to ask if there is anything the children want to share with the whole group at this point or you may want to leave it and stay with the topic. This is a judgement that is usually determined by the type and amount of talk going on in the pairs.

Next, tell the children to take it in turns to tell each other everything they know about Egypt. Remind them of their roles; speaker to speak, listener to encourage and draw out. They should be able to tell you about open questions, paraphrases, comments like 'Well you know loads don't you' to praise and encourage. Tell them they have about five minutes each. With older children this time may as much as fifteen minutes each, with younger ones five minutes between them. Praise any children with emotional and behavioural difficulties for their good listening or drawing out behaviour.

Now ask the children to join with another pair, to make a four. Encourage them to work with children they don't know too well, if they are in same gender pairs make sure they are in mixed gender fours, so that they have an opportunity to form a working relationship with every member of the class, regardless of gender, ethnic background or ability. Tell the children that you want them to share all the ideas from the two pairs, and to record these ideas on the sugar paper. Make it clear to the children that this recording can be pictures, drawings or symbols instead of - or as well as - words and they will probably enter into the activity with enthusiasm.

The brain-storm sheets can then be displayed; either in the classroom or in the hall where there is more room, and the children can then look at each others' and comment on how much they know already about Eygpt. They are often pleasantly surprised at the amount they know collectively.

It may be useful to mention to them that what they were doing when they found out from each other what they knew, was interviewing, and to explore the word interview and ask for examples.

> **Activity** - Using historical sources
>
> **Special needs context** - emotional and behavioural difficulty
> **Curriculum content** - history: using artifacts and
>   secondary sources
> **Skills** - interviewing

For the next session the teacher will need to sort out all the resources they have gathered onto tables of topics to make work stations. There should be at least two stations for each topic, and seating for at least two people. The topic headings could include: food and farming, pharaohs, gods, deaths and burials, religious beliefs, everyday life (past), hieroglyphics, building temples, everyday life today. Children seem to be fascinated by the details of ritual in the mummification process so several groups can easily do this topic and still come up with different pieces of information. For very young children who cannot read very well yet, the resources need to be visual or tactile; museum services can often help here.

Explain to the children that they are going to be researchers and explore the word with them. Tell them that they are going to work in pairs to find out some information, then join with another pair who have looked at the same topic, and interview each other. To get them into random pairs they could work with the person next to them to design a pair of cards that match; for example a drawing of a pyramid and the word pyramid. You can then collect in the cards, re-allocate them and use the cards again straight away to form pairs for the topic work. Again if you stress the importance of recording in any way they like, i.e., drawings, symbols, flow charts, diagrams, stick people, labels, when they do their research this usually results in a considerable amount of interest and enthusiasm.

Teacher behaviour here is very important. Whilst it would be counter-productive to refuse to help children who get stuck with a word, or do not understand a concept, it is helpful to combine responding behaviour with redirecting behaviour. If, for example, one of the children with emotional and behavioural difficulties is a good drawer, or has grasped the mummification process in some detail, that child can be treated as a consultant and other children directed to them. The same is true for spellings. The effects of being allocated such roles of responsibility are usually very positive as children with emotional and behavioural difficulties are well used to leading but usually in a negative rather than a positive way.

Teacher behaviour can be used in another way. There may be moments when your help is not needed and you can watch the group working, observe them, and comment on behaviours that they have been asked to demonstrate. This is also an ideal opportunity to use teacher praise to reward children, especially those with emotional and behavioural difficulties, who are working co-operatively with others, and particularly if they are helping others; for example those who struggle with their reading.

Once the pairs have finished their research — and this may take several sessions, especially if they get absorbed in it — they need to be moved to their fours and given instructions on interviewing. The interviewing in this case will consist of one pair taking it in turns to both draw out and summarise the contributions of the other pair.

Activity - Making an information poster

Special needs context - emotional and behavioural difficulty
Curriculum content - history and English AT1 and AT3,4,5
Skill - asking questions

Explain to the children that they are to gather together as much information about their topic as they can so that they can tell the others in the class about it. They will make a poster of their information after they have finished their interview. Tell them that you are going to come round and listen for turn taking, summarising and linking statements. Check to make sure that they all understand those terms. Give them about 20 minutes to do their interviewing and

20 minutes to do the poster. They then need to rehearse who is going to say what in the presentation.

For the presentation circle you will need enough pieces of paper or card for each child to have a piece of paper with a large question mark on to represent long questions, probably open questions, and two with small question marks on to represent short, probably closed questions. The presentation circle may take place on another session, in which case the children need an opportunity to rehearse or revise in their fours again.

When they are sitting in the circle in their fours, with one person from each group holding their poster, you can give out the question marks and explain the system to the children. They are only allowed to ask three questions each. When they ask their question they must say immediately whether it is a long one or a short one and put their piece of paper with the question mark in the middle of the circle. Each person must use their question. In our experience this technique serves two functions: it enables the children who usually dominate the talk to be controlled, and encourages them to use their talk to help the quieter ones to formulate questions; and it ensures that everyone listens and learns from the presentations other than their own, instead of presenting theirs, then switching off and wriggling about.

Once they have presented to each other you can ask for any

Figure 7:1 Children using 'question marks' to interview in a small circle

comments or anything they need clarifying and then suggest that they do a drama presentation of the mummification process for assembly. They can either be organised into groups to deal with different stages or they can sort themselves out, depending on the age and experience of the children. Children with emotional and behavioural difficulties can be given an organisational role at this point, for example being in charge of the props. The assembly presentation is another good opportunity to check speaking and listening skills. Many children end up mumbling so that their words are inaudible, or they read from a piece of paper and there is no feeling in what they are saying. Feedback is essential here if children are to improve. A useful way to get children to improve on their skills is video a rehearsal, then get the children to watch themselves and perhaps rate themselves on a self-assessment sheet on criteria such as, speaks loudly, speaks clearly, looks up, makes eye contact with the audience, smiles, puts feeling in what they are saying. This can then be followed up with a video of the actual assembly.

Another useful application of the interviewing technique is to arrange a visit to a local museum which has artifacts from Eygpt and arrange for either the museum curator, education worker or a local historian with a special knowledge of Eygpt to be interviewed by the children. They can prepare their questions in fours and then liaise with other groups to ensure that there is not too much repetition. This form of group interview, including introductions and thank yous, is a useful skill for the children to acquire for other subjects and again provides opportunities for responsibility to be offered to those with behavioural difficulties.

The Eygpt topic can be rounded off with a pair exercise on 'what I know about Eygpt now', with the children taking it in turns to review their learning and then, with the help of useful paraphrases from their partner, filling in a self-assessment grid based on National Curriculum criteria for history but written in children's phrases. Such grids along with photographs of the posters, can be kept in the record of achievement folder.

If you are able to plan in a cross-curricula way there are some excellent links with other subjects for the topic Eygpt; models of pyramids or sarcophagi for maths and technology, working out where Eygpt is and how you might get there, and looking at the African connections for geography, stories of being lost in museums or the curse of the mummy for English. Throughout this kind of work children can be encouraged to use their group skills and can conclude sections of work with self-assessment grids.

CHAPTER 8

Helping and Children with Special Needs

Self disclosure in the classroom

Teachers are all aware that in order to know how best to teach, motivate or discipline a child, they must first get to know what makes them tick. Teachers listen to what children say, observe them in the classroom and talk to them about their behaviour. The more a teacher does this then the more closely they can match the curriculum and the classroom to the needs of that child.

For children with special needs, those with learning difficulties and particularly those with behavioural problems, this 'finding out what makes them tick' is particularly important. These are the children who often seem to respond differently to teachers' strategies. As we have discussed previously they are also children who often have a poor image of themselves and low self-esteem. Understanding how best to approach these children's learning needs may not be simple or straightforward, as it involves the children's perceptions of themselves built up through a wide variety of experience outside the present teachers' knowledge.

For most teachers finding out about the children's thoughts and feelings, so as to better understand their motivation, is a rather ad hoc affair. The authors of this book believe that this can be more effectively achieved if the teacher structures activities which allow children to talk about themselves. This would include talking about their academic strengths and weaknesses, their aspirations, their hobbies and their families. These are topics that most teachers feel quite comfortable in tackling in the classroom. Indeed, it is clearly part of the open curriculum in the primary school.

The importance of talking about feelings

The curriculum in school, both the National Curriculum and the wider curriculum, aims to give children a broad and balanced education. However, when we look at the diet offered to most children in school, with or without special needs, it becomes quite clear that the way in which the curriculum is delivered in most part seeks to enhance and therefore use the children's academic skills. This ignores a great deal of the children's more creative, artistic and imaginative skills and abilities. It has been recognised for a long time that children need their physical well being taken into account so exercise in school is a normal and necessary part of the school curriculum. Teachers of very young children also recognise and advocate the role of imaginative play for learning.

For children with special needs it is vitally important that teachers utilise all of the children's abilities to enhance and ensure motivation, interest and learning. Branches of education and nursing who are dealing with children with profound and multiple learning difficulties children advocate the use of exercises which stimulate undamaged and unused areas of the brain to help those children to make progress. Within schools it has too long been the case that the more imaginative and creative aspects of the brain are not utilised in order to help children learn, for both the academic and the creative curriculum.

Those children who are relatively successful in school also need to have all aspects of their person stimulated and catered for within the school environment. A diet of reading, writing and recording is bound to become dry and un-stimulating even if you are successful and able to perform these tasks with ease.

The English writing attainment target for level 4 expects children to write about the way that characters feel in situations. In order to do this children need to have explored their own feelings and learnt to express them through the spoken or written word. They also need to have heard others use language to express their feelings, both to gain an understanding of what others mean by the same language and to gain an empathy with others' thoughts and feelings.

The authors feel that it vital that teachers allow children to talk about their feelings as a valid part of their life experience. This is often a neglected area in the school curriculum. It is too often left to the hidden curriculum of the classroom or left to children chatting in the playground. Unfortunately, when left to the arena of the playground children's feelings might not be dealt with sensitively. Experience tells us that hurt feelings are often the root of name calling, bullying and fighting.

Talking about feelings can actually cause people to experience those feelings again. This might explain why some teachers are reluctant to bring feelings into the classroom. It would seem that because children talking about feelings can be difficult for teachers, the more structure given to both the children and the teacher, the more able both parties are to deal with the accompanying emotions that are bound to be involved. The activity below provides a flexible structure which allows children to reveal as much or as little as they feel able. Classes who have done a lot of work on trust and sharing will find it easier to share their feelings. Classes where there is as yet not such a positive ethos may find that the activity in itself encourages disclosure and builds understanding, empathy and trust.

Roles in groups

This activity is one which is carried out in a group. The problems associated with groupwork are not fully explored here but the structures outlined in the previous chapters will have given the children some group skills which they can use in this activity. Children can be given the opportunity at this point of taking on specific roles within the group, starting with the simplest to identify, e.g. the leader or the scribe.

When the groups are selected, teachers may wish to use cards which designate a scribe and a group leader. This ensures that different children get an opportunity to take on these roles throughout the year. This is very important for children with special needs as they are likely to be those who would not normally be chosen, in the belief that leadership roles will be too difficult for them. For many children this might initially be the case, as they have been given little opportunity and practice in those roles.

Awarding these powerful group roles in advance has the advantage of keeping the group on task. Teachers should make sure that each role is clearly understood. The leader's task is to give everybody the opportunity to speak. Leaders should understand that their views are less important than the way in which they include all the other group members. By giving the task of writing down the list to a person other than the leader, the power roles are shared within the group. By making inclusion a specific task of the leader the situation where one child dominates the group is avoided.

Activity - Exploring feelings

Special needs context - hearing impaired
Curriculum content - English
Skill - talking about feelings

Organise the children into random or friendship groups of six. Each group is to divide into three pairs. Ask each pair to sit together and try to think of all the words they know that would describe a feeling. This process ensures that all the children are prepared for the next part of the activity, which involves writing (which can be stressful for many children). This verbal rehearsal is very useful to children with special needs and for those with a hearing impairment as it gives an opportunity for them to practise speaking the words they will later be expressing in a larger group situation. This built in practice time, with a one-to-one peer situation is very valuable to all those children who find hearing or speaking difficult.

Give the children a large sheet of paper and felt tip pens or crayons. Make sure that every child has something to write with. Tell them that they have just a few minutes to write or draw as many feelings as they can. Single words, phrases, symbols (such as a frowning face) can be given as examples. Each child is to write down as many feelings as they can. For children with hearing impairment this structure allows them to participate fully in the brain-storm activity, without having to concentrate on listening or speaking.

Afterwards, each group is to look at their sheet and make a joint list of the feelings which they wrote down. From that list they are to group together feelings that have been described in different words and to find a word which would describe the group. It may be that a group such as pleased, contented, cheerful, and happy could all be described as happy. This should reduce the list of feelings to some key words.

The groups can now either join together with another group or continue to work alone. They should be asked to decide on the six most common words for describing their feelings. Each member of the group now draws or writes one feeling on to a square of card. These cards are them taped together to form a 'feely dice'.

The creation of the net of a cube is part of the maths National Curriculum. Other solid shapes with flat surfaces can be used as well. Each group might be a different size and be given a different solid shape to made into a 'feely dice'.

The importance of allowing the children to generate the words for these feelings ensures that the words being used are understood by the children. It is possible, however, with young children or those with difficulties in writing, for the teacher to produce key words and pictures to illustrate feelings for the children to use. Some teachers may even wish to begin the activity by allowing the children to use a prepared feelings dice, in a simplified form. The one shown in figure 8.1 was made with tactile smiling and sad faces for use with a mixed blind, visually impaired and sighted group of children.

The groups can now work as groups of six or join together into twelves or even continue as a whole class using each of the dice in turn. The children throw the dice and use the picture or word to provide a stem statement for them to complete, e.g. *A time when I was angry was when* ... Children can share their experiences at whatever level they feel comfortable. Some may start off with trivial incidents whilst others might reveal feelings that are quite deep and profound. No child will risk any more than they are comfortable with, although there may be times when the teacher feels uncomfortable with what they hear. On future occasions the groups can swap their dice and use each others'.

Smaller groups take less time to complete the task and are possibly less threatening for children who have difficulties with hearing and speaking. Larger groups take more time but have the advantage of allowing the children to listen to a greater number of contributors and increase their understanding and empathy towards more of the class. This activity could be varied, beginning with small groups and moving towards the whole class situation, over time. It is a good idea in the whole class circle if the teacher joins in and takes their turn at sharing their feelings with the children.

A follow up activity for the class could be a class feeling book or posters where children write about or draw pictures of the incidents that they have talked about in the circle.

Figure 8:1 Net for a 'feely' dice

Asking for help

If children are used to talking about how they feel then the steps of identifying feelings of helplessness and then asking for help will be made easier. All children need help at some time or another, with things they learn. When and how to help any child is a decision made many times a day by parents and teachers. If you don't allow a child to try for themselves they will never learn to do anything for themselves. They need to 'go it alone' to demonstrate to themselves their own ability and success. If you don't ever help them or leave them to struggle for too long they will constantly feel as if they are failing and never want to try to do anything new again. This will effectively prevent them learning.

Children with special needs are often being helped in one way or another. There are times when those children may want to try for themselves and they are helped before they would wish. This might often be the case as children with difficulties in school might be cushioned against 'failure' by an over-eager wish to support and help. On other occasions they might need help but not receive it. If the child learns to cover up their failures by disruptive behaviours, copying from others, living down to low expectations or using other 'survival strategies' they might well not get the help they need, as the teacher will be led to believe they don't really need it.

Although all children need help, children with special needs are perhaps those for whom prior expectations and experience will prevent them from asking for the help they need. All the children in a class can benefit from looking at the ways to ask for help and examining the language which they can use to refuse help when it is not needed.

The question arises of whom to ask for help. The teacher (or other adult) is normally the one from whom help is forthcoming in the classroom. This means that for some children the amount of help that can be given is very small. Children with learning difficulties, who do not have special help within the classroom, might suffer from the lack of individual help and support in mainstream classrooms. Children with physical differences might find it difficult to constantly have to ask an adult for help to reach an object, write or type, go to the toilet or eat, provided there is an adult there for them. Even if ancillaries and support teachers are working with the class teacher they are of limited numbers. They are also inclined to change at the end of a year, or in secondary schools at the end of each teaching period.

The peer group of the child, however, is usually constant, and in many cases these children are with them throughout years of schooling. If the children are taught how to ask their own peers for appropriate help then they need make less demands on the teacher. The peer group needs to be taught how to give that help in the way that best suits them both. As the peer group becomes accustomed to giving the support asked for, some of the barriers between students with special needs and those in mainstream are broken down. They are also more able to work towards independence, with support only when asked for.

An important aspect of teaching children to ask for help is to ensure that students who may have obvious special needs are also asked for help in areas where they may have strengths, where mainstream pupils do not. It may be that the student with special needs uses a piece of equipment or a sign language such as Makaton, which they can be asked to teach to another mainstream student. They might be very talented in a particular way, e.g. musically gifted, artistic or mathematical. Their talents can be used to help the other students in the class. The reciprocal nature of asking for help as well as practising the forms of words to use is very important for the self-esteem of students with special needs, who might well have never been in the position of giving help to others, only receiving it.

In a circle ask the children to sit and think for a moment of times when they have asked for help or been asked for help. Allow a verbal brain-storm or allow the children to go in turns around the circle and write down the list as it's given to you on a large sheet of paper. Repeats of situations can be tallied against the first one mentioned. When a list has been generated ask the children to take a card and either draw, write or both, as appropriate, situations where you might ask for help. Children may work in pairs to do this if that is appropriate or be asked to do this individually. Put the cards into bag or box and then invite each child or pair to pick out a card at random. Each child goes around the room (rather like at a party) spots someone who is alone at that moment, goes up to them and asks for help, pretending to be in the situation that the card describes. The other person needs to pick up what the situation is and respond appropriately. It might help the children if the teacher picks out a card at random and goes up to one of the students and role plays that situation. For example:

Hello. I'm in a bit of a mess and I wonder if you could help me. I've got a flat tyre and I can't remove the wheel nuts. Could you help me to move them or make a phone call to my friend who would come and help me?

Yes, of course. I'm afraid I'm not very strong myself, but I'll come and try and if we can't do it together then I'll make that phone call for you. You look tired, would you like to come in for a cup of tea before we start?

They can then role play the other person's card. When they have finished the short role play they move on to the next person they see alone. This way they can practise their roles and try out different ways of asking for help, and giving it. After two or three goes the cards can be returned and a different situation card taken by each person.

It is possible for the teacher to create the cards ready for this activity, or have cards with phrases or mini- scripts for the students to practise, e.g. 'Excuse me, would you help me onto the bus, please.' 'I'm finding this maths a bit difficult, can you explain this to me again.' 'This bit doesn't make sense to me, can we read it together.' etc.

If the children work in pairs each pair can take a card other than their own and role play that situation and then reverse the roles. The cards can be swapped about as before.

At the end of this activity it will be important to allow the whole group ten minutes to talk about how they felt when they were in role. This debriefing of their feelings is a very important aspect of learning that it is O.K. to ask for help and give it. Children with special needs will need to know that everyone feels a bit shy or awkward when requesting help at first and that this is not something that they alone feel. You might do this as a whole class circle or in smaller circles of about eight children. Stress that the children need to talk about their feelings when they asked for help and their feelings afterwards, not just what happened and what was said.

Using mime in encouraging children to ask for help

For children with special needs the act of asking for help can be one with which they are very familiar. They might not, however, be used to being asked for help. The following activity uses role play to allow children to understand the difficulties that their peers might have and to practise ways in which they can both ask for and respond to requests for help.

Activity - Mime of 'helping'

Special needs context - hearing impaired
Curriculum content - English
Skill - the language of asking for help

Prepare stickers which have different situations on them and stick them onto the children's backs. These might be activities like making a cup of tea, washing up, going out at playtimes, going to the park, or they might be school based activities like drawing a circle using a pin and string, mounting pictures, loading a kiln, tidying a bookshelf, using balance scales etc. Ask the children to get into pairs and for one to read the sticker on the other one's back. For children who can't read the teacher can use pictures of the task. The child should then mime the actions of the task using gestures and facial expressions as well as body movements. Their partner is to guess what is on their back. However, the children should not say what they think their sticker is until the end of this section of the activity.

Teachers should set a time limit on each mime so that children don't feel frustrated by failing to guess. The roles should then be reversed. Children then should move on to new partners and repeat the activity two or three times. At this point they should remove their sticker and see whether their guess was right.

Teachers might point out the importance of making clear gestures to help other people understand what you are speaking about. This is particularly important if the special needs of some of the children are hearing impairment.

Once the children have identified the sticker on their back, ask them to move to a new partner. This time the partner is not allowed to look at the task. The child should mime asking for help with their own task to this new partner. The partner should not try to guess as such but join in the mime as the 'helper'.

Following the activity the teacher should ask the children how it felt to be without the verbal prompts and allow the children to share the things which helped them to join in and those that didn't. The feelings of helping and being asked for help can also be explored. Helping in the academic subjects in the classroom can then be discussed. This can be seen as an extension of helping and no longer regarded as 'cheating'.

Giving feedback on helpfulness

Once they have explored the nature and language of asking for help and the feelings associated with the giving and receiving of help, the incidence of children helping each other will increase. The powerful tool of teacher approval will also help to increase helpful behaviours, both in academic and social areas. Once children are helping each other then the class can explore the best ways in which they can help each other.

Giving feedback is a high level skill which will need further work than this book can allow. The aspect of giving feedback here is concerned with the particular effect of giving feedback about how well a person has helped another. This provides the opportunity for students with special needs to express their feelings about what sort of help they desire and need and what help is actually experienced as interference and so is not helpful at all.

As with all feedback, the more specific it is the more useful it is. The following activity can follow an asking for help exercise, but it can be adapted to allow pupils to give peer group feedback on other aspects of supportive behaviour in the classroom, such as 'making me feel wanted', 'being friendly', 'teaching me things', 'listening to me' etc.

By giving a structure to feedback on these aspects the teacher raises the students' awareness of what sort of behaviour is needed. It gives an opportunity for students to find out how their behaviour is perceived by others. This feedback also gives them a picture of what they could and should be doing and allows them to make changes to their behaviour in very specific ways. The structure also allows teachers the opportunity to notice, acknowledge and praise behaviours which she/he would wish to encourage. These may relate to incidents which may not otherwise have been seen by the teacher.

Activity - Giving feedback on 'helping'

Special needs context - hearing impaired
Curriculum content - English
Skill - giving appropriate help

Give out sets of numbered coloured cards. Playing cards are particularly useful for this. Children are to find someone who has the same suit (or colour) as they have. Ask the children to sit with that person and talk about a time that they remember noticing something helpful that the other person did, either for them or for another person that they know. Ask each child to summarise what the other has said (see chapter five).

The children then move to one other person in their 'suit' or colour and talk to them about a time when that person was helpful to them. The cards can be structured to help the children decide on their first pair, second pair etc. It might help the children for the teacher to illustrate by saying, 'A time when I remember John being helpful was when he opened the door for me when it was raining and I'd got all those books to carry.' John might be asked to summarise by using a phrase that includes 'I'. This might be, 'I was helpful when I opened the door.'

The children should then be asked to go randomly about their set of people, which will give them the opportunity to both give and receive feedback and summarise using 'I' statements four or five times.

Having received this feedback the children should join with their partner in another set (e.g. the two of hearts with the two of diamonds, the two of spades with the two of clubs). They then take it in turns to describe themselves by their helpful behaviours, which have been fed back to them by the group. Alternatively, the children can use the party structure to give feedback to each other, beginning each statement with, 'Thank you for helping me with ... when you ...'

Children might feel strange doing these activities as boasting is often frowned upon and being thanked is a rare occurrence in schools! When vocalising these statements children are helped to recognise which behaviours are seen by others as 'good'. This can lead to a desire to perform more of these helpful or good behaviours.

The vocalising and public nature of these acclamations are one way in which children with a low self-esteem can begin to attribute positive qualities to themselves. This is vital in breaking the negative low self-esteem cycle that is common for many children with special needs. As children get more experienced at giving feedback the same structures can be used to give a balance of both negative and positive feedback to children, helping them to move away from unhelpful or negative behaviours.

Conclusion

The authors of this book have successfully taught mixed groups of children using the strategies outlined. Throughout our work as teacher trainers many other teachers have reported to us that by using these methods their teaching has been revitalised, their classroom climate has become more positive and their children have achieved more academic success than before.

Teachers talk with amazement and awe at the level of empathy, care and concern that children can show, one for the other. The football hero of the top year sitting in the library with a reception child on his knee reading stories, the blind girl running hand in hand through the woodland with a sighted peer while orienteering, the year three boy who crossed the sharing circle to comfort a girl whose father had just left home because he had shared that experience, saying "I know how you feel because that happened to me too".

These are the teachers who have asked for this book to be written.

Whilst this book is comprehensive in its coverage of the skills, the examples given are necessarily limited to a particular curriculum content and special needs context. These are intended as examples only. Teachers using this book might wish to begin by following the suggestions as if it is a prescriptive programme in order to gain experience and confidence in working this way.

Some teachers may prefer to begin by taking just one curriculum area. One teacher of year six children took the curriculum subjects of Maths and English and spent two terms working through all the skills from non-verbal communication skills through to expression of feeling and giving feedback. This teacher found that, with very little alteration to the actual lesson structure, most of the examples given could be readily transferred to these particular subject areas.

Other teachers, particularly of younger children, may wish to spend more time building up their non-verbal skills, their initial verbal skills and their skills in talking effectively. One teacher of year one children took a whole term working through all the various curriculum areas, in order to teach and reinforce the children's eye contact and non verbal behaviour, concentrating on pair and circle work alone.

By working through the programme teachers should gain an understanding of the progression of skills necessary for children to work effectively with each other, in pairs, as peer tutors and in groups. Once teachers have grasped the ordering of the skills we hope that they will transfer the skills to other curriculum areas and adapt them for other special needs contexts. These are infinite in their variety and will be tailored by teachers to fit their own children and class groups.

Through the teaching of skills as outlined in this book the needs of all children can be met.

We believe that for children with special needs this is not only convenient - it is vital.

Bibliography

Abramson, L.Y., Seligman, M.E.P. and Teasdale, J. (1978) 'Learned Helplessness in Humans: Critique and Reformulation' *Journal of Abnormal Psychology*, **87**, 49-74.

Alexander, R., Rose, J., Woodhead, C. (1992) *Curriculum Organisation and Classroom Practice in Primary Schools: a discussion paper* The 'three wise men' report (London: D.E.S.).

Barnes, D. (1977) *From Communication to Curriculum* (Harmondsworth: Penguin).

Bennett et al (1976) *Teaching styles and pupil progress* (London: Open Books).

Bloom, B.S. (1984) 'The Search for Methods of Group Instruction as Effective as One to One Tutoring' *Educational Leadership*, May, 4-17

Booth, T., Potts, P. and Swann, W. (1987) *Preventing Difficulties in Learning* (Oxford: Basil Blackwell).

Bruner, J.S. (1986) *Actual Minds, Possible Words* Howard Press.

Burns, R. (1982) *Self Concept Development and Education* (New York: Holt, Reinhart and Winston).

Chapman, J.W. Lamborne, R. and Silva, P.A. (1990) 'Some Antecedents of Academic Self Concept: A Longitudinal Study' *British Journal of Educational Psychology*, **60**, 142-152.

Craske, M.L. (1988) 'Learned Helplessness, Self Worth Motivation and Attribution Retraining for Primary School Children' *British Journal of Educational Psychology*.

Coopersmith, S. (1967) *Antecedents of Self Esteem* (San Francisco: W.H. Freeman and Co.).

Cottle, T.J. (1965) 'Self Concept, Ego Ideal and the Response to Action' *Social Society Research* **50**, 78-88.

Dessant, T. (1987) *Making the Ordinary School Special* London: Falmer Press

Flanders, N. (1970) *Analyzing Teacher Behaviour* (Addison Wesley).

Galton, Simon and Croll (1980) *Inside the Primary Classroom* (London Routledge and Kegan Paul).

Goodlad, S. and Hirst, B. (1989) *Peer Tutoring: A Guide to Learning by Teaching* (London: Kogan Page).

Gordan, T. (1974) *T.E.T. Teacher Effectiveness Training* (New York: Peter Wyden).

Gray, J. and Richer, J. (1988) *Classroom Resposes to Disruptive Behaviour* (Basingstoke: MacMillan).

Gurney, P.W. (1988) *Self-Esteem in Children with Special Educational*

Needs (London: Routledge).

Hamachek, D.E. (1986) (3rd edition) *Encounters with Self* (New York: Holt, Reinhart and Winston).

Lalkhen, Y. and Norwich, B. (1990) 'The Self Concept and Self Esteem of Adolescents with Physical Impairments in Integrated and Special School Settings' *European Journal of Special Needs*, 5, No1.

Lawrence, D. (1987) *Enhancing Self Esteem in the Classroom* (Paul Chapman Publishing Co.).

Lawrence, D. (1973) *Improved Reading through Counselling* (London: Ward Lock).

Lewis, A.R. (1971) 'The Self Concept of Adolescent ESN boys' *British Journal of Educational Psychology*, 41, 222-223.

Lund, R. (1987) 'The Self Esteem of Children with Emotional and Behavioural Difficulties' *Maladjustment and Theraputic Education*, 5, No 1.

Piaget, J. (1959) *Language and Thought of the Child* (London: Routledge and Kegan Paul).

Rosenthal, R. and Jacobson, L. (1968) *Pygmallion in the Classroom: Teacher Expectaion and Pupils' Intellectual Development* (New York: Holt, Rinehart and Winston).

Skaalvik, E.M. (1990) 'Attributions of Percieved Academic Results and Relations with Self Esteem in Senior High Schools' *Scandinavian Journal of Educational Research*, 34, No 4.

Skinner, B.F. (1969) *Contingencies of Reinforcement: A theoretical Analysis* (New York: Appleton Century Crofts).

Sutton, C. (Ed) (1981) *Communicating in the Classroom: A guide for subject teachers on the more effective use of reading, writing and talk* (London: Hodder and Stoughton).

Swann (1988) in Thomas, G. and Feiler, A. (Eds) (1988) *Planning for Special Needs* (Oxford: Blackwell).

Tann, S. (1991) *Developing Language in the Primary Classroom* (London: Cassell).

Thomas, G. and Feiler, A. (Eds) (1988) *Planning for Special Needs* (Oxford: Blackwell).

Topping, K. (1988) *The Peer Tutoring Handbook* (London: Croom Helm).

Vygotsky, L.S. (1987) *Thought and Language* (Cambridge, Mass:MIT Press).

Wells, G. (1985) *Language and Learning: an interactive perspective* (Lewes: Falmer Press).

Wells, G. (1986) *Meaning Makers - Children Learning Language and Using Language to Learn* (London: Hodder and Stoughton).

White, M. (1990) 'Circle time' *Cambridge Journal of Education*, 20, No 1.

Whylie, R.C. (1979) *The Self Concept* Vol 2, University of Nabraska, Lincoln.

R

The South East Essex
College of Arts & Technology
Carnarvon Road   Southend on Sea   Essex   SS2 6LS
Tel: Southend (0702) 220400   Fax: Southend (0702) 432320